Felix Mendelssohn

His Life, His Family, His Music

BY HERBERT KUPFERBERG

Illustrated with Photographs and Prints

Charles Scribner's Sons · New York

Printed in the United States of America
Library of Congress Catalog Card Number 72–1172
SBN 684–12952–3 (cloth, RB)

To Seth, Joel, and Natalie

Contents

List of Illustrations

Introduction

On the surface, the life of Felix Mendelssohn is a musical success story. How else can you describe the career of a composer who achieved fame while still in his teens, who never had financial worries, and who was the musical idol of two countries, Germany and England?

And yet, despite his outward successes, Felix Mendelssohn was a young man who knew strife, struggle, and tragedy. His own life, and that of many in his family, was cut short by sudden and unexpected death. He lived at a time when new artistic currents were flowing strongly, and he had to fight to maintain his own musical integrity among them. And as long as he lived, he had to contend with some unusual personal problems and doubts.

Some of his troubles stemmed from his family heritage. Felix Mendelssohn was born a Jew. His grandfather, Moses Mendelssohn, had been the foremost Jewish leader in Europe —a philosopher who helped emancipate his people from their ignorance and isolation. But Felix's father turned his children into Christians, giving them a divided loyalty that pursued them all their lives.

In this book I have tried to tell how Felix faced up to his artistic and personal challenges and overcame them. The tales of his feats as a child prodigy and his composition of the

Midsummer Night's Dream Overture at the age of seventeen are well known. But not so familiar are his wanderings through Europe as a young man with a taste for new experiences and an eye for the girls, or his accomplishments as the central musical personality of his time, flourishing simultaneously as conductor, composer, and pianist.

Not the least fascinating aspect of the story, I have found, is the extraordinary Mendelssohn family, the remarkable parents, sisters, and brother who joined in Felix's adventures and shared his triumphs and, in the end, his tragedy. Few musical families, in my opinion, achieved more together in their lifetimes, or are more worth knowing today.

Felix Mendelssohn

His Life, His Family, His Music

The Grandfather

———⟨∞⟩———

In September of 1743, a fourteen-year-old boy carrying his belongings in a small pack on his back walked eighty miles from the town of Dessau in central Germany to Berlin, the capital of the kingdom of Prussia. He was small, humpbacked, and spoke with a stammer. His name, taken from his native city, was Moses Dessau. Few people who passed him during the five days he walked on that dusty road could have regarded him as a figure of much importance. Yet, under the name of Moses Mendelssohn, he was to become one of the most famous men of his time, as well as the grandfather of a great composer, Felix Mendelssohn.

As Moses approached Berlin he headed for a checkpoint called the Rosenthaler Gate. He did so because he was Jewish, and this was the only entrance into Berlin open to Jews. In fact, the Jews of the city posted their own watchman there to make sure that beggars or people without means did not enter. But Moses was lucky. When the guard asked him why he had come to Berlin, he blurted out the words: "To learn." The watchman laughed. "Go, Moses," he said with an ironic wave, "the sea has opened before you."

Actually Moses had been doing little else besides learning during his young lifetime—but it was learning of a very particular and limited kind. Born on September 6, 1729, into a poor family, he lived in a crowded and squalid ghetto. The school he went to was a religious institution, conducted in the Yiddish language and held in a dark, bare room of the local synagogue. His father, Mendel Dessau, who was a religious scribe himself, would awaken Moses at three or four in the morning, wrap an old cloak about him, and carry him through the streets to the daily class led by a bearded rabbi. Most of the instruction dealt with the intricacies of Jewish ritual and doctrine rather than with the beauty, philosophy, and drama of the Jews' incomparable literary legacy, the Old Testament. It was not a very stimulating curriculum.

But Moses' active mind soon found more interesting reading matter in the form of a book called *A Guide to the Perplexed* written in 1190 by a Jewish philosopher named Maimonides. It was a book written to answer the doubts of those who were puzzled by the Bible and to bridge the gap between religion and reason. Although it is still read today, it has always been a difficult book. Young Moses plunged into it eagerly and pored over it night after night by an oil lamp. He had always been frail and undersized, but now as he repeatedly turned its thousand pages, his spine developed a permanent curvature. "Maimonides gave me my hump," he later said ruefully, "but although he weakened my body, he invigorated my soul."

At thirteen Moses underwent his bar mitzvah ritual in the local synagogue. Today this ceremony merely symbolizes the entry of a Jewish boy into manhood. In those days its meaning was much more literal, for at thirteen childhood was considered really over, and a youth was expected to begin working for a living.

What was a boy like Moses to do? Jews at that time were legally restricted from entering most of the trades and professions, just as they were barred from living anywhere than ghettos. Moses, small and spindly as he was, seemed unfit for manual or heavy labor. The only trade open to him was that of a peddler—carting a sack of clothing or household articles from village to village and selling this merchandise to house-wives. It was not a prospect that pleased him. His function in life, as he told the guard at the Rosenthaler Gate, was "to learn." And the place to do this was Berlin, where the court of King Frederick the Great glittered, and where scholars from all of Germany congregated.

To a stooped and stammering boy from Dessau, Berlin seemed a bewildering city. But Moses found friends there —Rabbi David Frankel, who was from Dessau himself and remembered him as a bright and willing pupil, and a Jew-ish merchant named Herman Bamberg, who gave him sleeping space in his attic plus an occasional meal.

The Talmud, which was one of the books young Moses had studied in Dessau, gives this advice to scholars: "Eat bread with salt, drink water by measure, sleep upon the hard earth, lead a life of privation, and busy thyself with the Law."

Not a very attractive prospect—but it describes pretty accurately how young Moses lived between the ages of fourteen and twenty-one. His basic diet for those years consisted of a loaf of bread which he bought each week and marked with seven notches, so that he could eat one portion daily. What little money he earned as a Hebrew scribe and copyist, he used to buy books.

Soon word began to spread through the Jewish commu-nity in Berlin of the eager young scholar from Dessau, and others began to assist him in his quest for knowledge. Latin he learned by himself, but a medical student he met taught him English and French. A Lutheran pastor who took an interest in him gave him Greek lessons. When a young mathematician arrived from Poland and sought lodgings in the Jewish quarter, Moses shared his garret with him—in return for lessons in logic and Euclidian geometry. Wrote Moses later on: "I have never been to a university, nor have I heard a classroom lecture, and one of the greatest difficulties I had to surmount was that I had to obtain everything by my own effort and industry."

So well versed did Moses become in all branches of learning that at the age of twenty-one he was engaged as a tutor for the four children of a wealthy Jewish merchant named Isaac Bernhard. This meant that he could give up his garret for a room in the Bernhard house and live in comparative comfort. So pleased was Bernhard with his new employee that he eventually took him into his silk business as a partner. All day long he sat in the silk factory, keeping the books, seeing customers, supervising the workers. But in his pocket he always carried a volume of poetry or philosophy to read in a spare moment, and at night he joined a circle of other

Moses Mendelssohn, grandfather of Felix. He left the Dessau ghetto at fourteen to become famous as a philosopher, author, and emancipator of the Jews.

young men for animated discussions of current literary, political, and intellectual happenings. Throughout his life, Moses found it possible to be a businessman by day and a philosopher by night.

In fact, he gradually launched himself on a flourishing career as a critic and writer. By now he had become a master of the German language. No Jew before him had ever used that tongue with such fluency and elegance. When he came to Berlin he decided to stop using the name Moses Dessau and to be known in the traditional Jewish manner as the son of his father. In Hebrew, this would have been "Moshe ben Mendel"—Moses, son of Mendel. Instead, he Germanicized the name to Moses Mendelssohn.

Many of Moses' Berlin friends were young Christians who were in the forefront of liberal thought of their day. Few of them had ever met a Jew before, and they were fascinated by the bright-eyed, hunched-over young philosopher from Dessau, who could discourse so brilliantly on so many subjects, and yet who remained so modest, unassuming, and openhearted.

Among these young friends was Gotthold Ephraim Lessing, a poet and playwright who was well connected in literary circles. Moses Mendelssohn had written a set of essays called *Philosophical Observations*, which he deferentially showed to Lessing one night, asking for his opinion of it. Lessing read it and, without telling Mendelssohn, quietly took it to his own publisher. Weeks went by, with Moses too timorous to remind his friend about the manuscript he had left with him. One night he got up enough courage to do so, and Lessing replied by handing him a printed copy of the book, which had just arrived, and a handful of ducats. "Here is your book," he said. "I am sorry I could not get more than this for it from the publisher."

With Lessing and others, Moses Mendelssohn formed a club called the Learned Coffee House, which met monthly in a café. They each took turns presenting a philosophical or mathematical paper. Since Mendelssohn had never lost his stammer, he usually asked another member to read his paper for him. Once, when each member was asked to make up a poem about his own personal defects, Mendelssohn wrote:

> *Great you call Demosthenes,*
> *Stuttering orator of Greece;*
> *Hunchback Aesop you deem wise—*
> *In your circle I surmise*
> *I am doubly wise and great.*
> *What in each was separate*
> *You in me united find—*
> *Hump and heavy tongue combined.*

In 1762, when Mendelssohn was thirty-three years old, he married a blonde, blue-eyed girl from Hamburg named Fromet Gugenheim. Although she knew of his reputation as a philosopher and had read some of his writings, she was shocked when she first saw his humpbacked figure. Seeing her distress, Moses sat down beside her and said to her gently, "Let me tell you a story. When a Jewish child is born, proclamation is made in heaven of the name of the person that he or she will some day marry. When I was born, my future wife was also named, but at the same time it was said that she herself would be humpbacked. 'O God,' I said, 'a deformed girl will lead an unhappy life. Dear Lord, give the humpback to me, and let the girl be flawless and beautiful.' " Tears came to Fromet's eyes, and a few months afterward they were married.

In 1767 Moses Mendelssohn wrote a book called *Phaedon* which made him famous throughout Europe. It was a modernization of the Greek philosopher Plato's account of the last day and execution of the great Athenian Socrates. So avid was the demand for it that it went through many editions and was

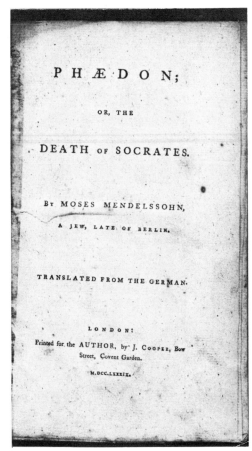

PHÆDON;

OR, THE

DEATH OF SOCRATES.

BY MOSES MENDELSSOHN,
A JEW, LATE OF BERLIN.

TRANSLATED FROM THE GERMAN.

LONDON:
Printed for the AUTHOR, by J. COOPER, Bow
Street, Covent Garden.

M.DCC.LXXXIX.

Moses Mendelssohn's *Phaedon* became the best-selling book of its day, with many translations from the original German. This is title page of English edition, published in 1789.

translated into every European language from English to Hungarian. People thought it especially remarkable that such a book, requiring a knowledge of Greek and an understanding of philosophy, should have been written by a Jew who had been raised in a ghetto and had never received a classical education. Moses' *Phaedon* even made its way to the court of Frederick the Great, king of Prussia, whose advisers—including a good many French expatriates like the great Voltaire—read it eagerly.

Moses also came to the attention of Frederick in another way, which might have had less pleasant consequences for him. With Lessing and other literary friends, he put out a periodical called *Letters About Literature* which reviewed the latest books and pamphlets. Frederick the Great, who fancied himself as a poet, had written a little volume of verse, in French, which Moses reviewed unfavorably. Some of the courtiers were angered that an unlettered Jew should have the temerity to criticize a king, and Moses was summoned to court to explain himself.

Appearing before the king in his plain, dark garments, Moses gravely said, "Your Majesty, writing poetry is like bowling. Whoever bowls, whether he be a king or a peasant, must have the pinboy tell him the score." The "explanation" must have satisfied the king, for he took no further action against Mendelssohn.

From that time on, stories began to spread about the supposed intimacy of Moses Mendelssohn with Frederick the Great. It seems doubtful that there was ever any great depth of sympathy between them; nevertheless the legends persisted in Jewish folklore. According to one story, Frederick summoned Moses to his palace to ask his advice on a matter of state. When he arrived at the gate, an officer, seeing his stooped figure and poor garments, stopped him haughtily and asked him what business he had with the king. "I am a juggler," replied Moses—and was promptly admitted. "But why did you tell him that?" asked the king later. "Because," said Moses, "I know it is easier for a juggler to get into your palace than a philosopher."

Another time Mendelssohn was supposed to have encountered the king and his retinue while out for a stroll on the street. "Good morning, Mr. Mendelssohn, where are you going?" asked the monarch. "I don't know," replied Mendelssohn. "How dare you make such an answer to me! Guard! Take this man to prison!" shouted the incensed Frederick. "You see, Your Majesty?" said Mendelssohn, as the guard prepared to lead him off. "Did I know I was going to prison?"

The king's anger turned to laughter, and he let him off.

When it came to serious affairs, Frederick the Great was not very inclined to show kindliness, or even tolerance, to his Jewish subjects. Severe limitations were placed on where they could live, what jobs they could hold, whether they could marry, how many children they could have. They were divided into three classifications called, in descending order, Court Jews, Protected Jews, and Tolerated Jews. Despite his eminence as a philosopher and scholar, Moses Mendelssohn remained in the lowest group, that of a Tolerated Jew, with no legal rights or protections at all. A Catholic philosopher, the Marquis d'Argens, tried to persuade the king to raise Mendelssohn at least one notch, and wrote the following graciously worded appeal: "A bad Catholic philosopher begs a bad Protestant philosopher to grant the Privilege [of being a Protected Jew] to a bad Jewish philosopher. There is too much philosophy in all this for the request not to be justified." Nevertheless, the king held back, and not for many years did Moses Mendelssohn receive his basic human rights.

Frederick the Great had a regulation which required every Jewish couple upon being married to make a large purchase from the royal porcelain works. He had established this factory to aid German industry, and forcing Jews to buy unwanted merchandise from it was a good way to help business. Usually the unwilling customers had to take whatever goods the plant manager wanted to get rid of. As a result, Moses and Fromet Mendelssohn became the reluctant owners of twenty large porcelain apes, which henceforth stood around their house in various nooks and crannies, becoming a family joke for years.

But the Mendelssohn house in Berlin became famous for another reason. Every night, when Moses returned home from his work at the silk factory, his living room was filled with friends, relatives, and visitors who came for an evening of philosophic conversation and discussion. By now Moses

Mendelssohn had become widely known as "the modern Plato" or "the German Socrates." Even travelers from abroad made it a point to pay a call at his house during their visits to Berlin. Fromet would put out plates of raisins and almonds, and sometimes a light supper. Moses would sit in his armchair as a kind of umpire for the discussions. Among his visitors were many Christians, curious to see the famous "Jew of Berlin." Some of them tried to engage him in religious debates, but he always gently declined, for he preferred to avoid controversy. At such moments he was fond of quoting the ancient Jewish sage Hillel, who, upon being asked to recite the essence of Judaism while standing on one foot, had replied: "Do not do unto others that which you would not have them do unto you. That is the entire Law; the rest is commentary."

But one of his distinguished Christian guests refused to be satisfied with that answer. His name was Johann Caspar Lavater, and he was a Protestant deacon from the city of Zurich in Switzerland. Lavater was a curious person. He had invented a "science" called "physiognomy" which, he said, enabled him to read a person's character by examining his facial features. In the case of Moses Mendelssohn, he announced that "the noble curve of his forehead" and "the prominent bones of the eye" proved that he had "a Socratic soul." Lavater also was an active proselytizer for Christianity —that is, he tried to convert members of other faiths to his religion. He had just translated from French into German a book called *Inquiry into the Evidences of Christianity*. He dedicated his translation to Moses Mendelssohn, and called on him either to refute the pro-Christian arguments in the book or to publicly renounce Judaism and accept conversion to Christianity.

Moses was horrified at this challenge—not because he had doubts about his own faith, but because he abhorred the idea of engaging in public religious controversy. Finally, however, he published his answer in the form of a pamphlet called *Letter to Johann Caspar Lavater* in which he affirmed the right of every man to practice his own religion as he saw fit. "I am as firmly convinced of the essentials of my religion as you, sir, are of yours," he wrote to Lavater, "and I herewith declare in the presence of the God of Truth, who has created us both, and in whose name you have challenged me, that I will hold to my principles as long as my soul remains unchanged."

So powerful was Mendelssohn's 4,000-word reply that Lavater immediately withdrew his challenge and apologized publicly. Congratulatory messages came to Mendelssohn from all over Europe, especially from people who believed, as he did, in religious liberty and freedom of conscience. Moses Mendelssohn suddenly became regarded as an embodiment of the democratic ideal.

He also became, to his own surprise, a spokesman for his own people. The Jews of Europe at that time had no leader, no advocate, no unified voice. In fact, they were hardly part of European civilization at all. They lived apart from the world around them, having little commerce or contact with non-Jews. True, there were a few who by dint of special talent or by sheer luck managed to establish themselves as bankers or businessmen and even performed special functions at royal courts. But the great bulk of Jews hardly knew any language but Yiddish. They read no books except Hebraic doctrinal commentaries like the Talmud. And they knew practically nothing of the great new ideals of democracy and freedom that were in the air. The ghetto walls which separated them physically from their neighbors also cut them off from the mainstream of European civilization.

Moses Mendelssohn was the first to cross the gap that separated eighteenth-century Jews from their Christian contemporaries. And, having done so himself, he decided to help others take the same step. He translated the Hebrew Bible into German, which led many young Jews to learn the German language, previously unknown to them. For many it made German rather than Yiddish their everyday tongue. He expressed his own original religious ideas in language that was clear and eloquent—the idea, for instance, that God was much more likely to judge men by what they *did* than by what they *believed.* Some of the more traditional rabbis were disturbed by the novelty of Mendelssohn's concepts, but the younger Jews of his day took them up eagerly, so that he became the leader of the Jewish Enlightenment. Moses remained an Orthodox, observant Jew to the end of his life. But after his death some of his followers decided to expand his idea that Jews should be part of the modern world. They began to change and eliminate some of the old religious rituals and customs, which they regarded as out of date. The result was a movement called Reform Judaism, which eventually was taken up by some American Jews.

Mendelssohn also began to exercise leadership in combatting injustices done to Jews in various parts of Europe. He appealed to King Louis XVI of France (later to be executed in the French Revolution) to ease the plight of Jews in Alsace who were burdened with heavy taxes and humiliating regulations. He persuaded several Swiss towns to lift restrictions against Jewish marriages. He interceded with the civil authorities of Dresden, who had ordered large numbers of Jews expelled. Jews from throughout Europe turned to "Reb Moshe," as they called him, whenever there was an injustice to correct or a wrong to right. And although he held no governmental position or any official status, his prestige and reputation were so great that the authorities were often willing to listen to him.

All the while Moses and Fromet Mendelssohn were raising their family. Three sons and three daughters were born to them; their second son, Abraham, was to become the father of Felix Mendelssohn. Together with his elder brother, Joseph, Abraham went into the banking business, establishing an institution, Mendelssohn and Company, that lasted until 1939, when the Nazis liquidated it. But whatever his sons did, Moses Mendelssohn cared little for making money. Philosophy, literature, and working for his fellow men remained his prime preoccupations to the end of his life.

In 1779, when Moses Mendelssohn was fifty years old, he unexpectedly became the hero of a stage play. His friend Lessing wrote *Nathan the Wise*, a drama about a Jewish merchant living in Jerusalem at the time of the Crusades. *Nathan the Wise* was Lessing's masterpiece and one of the most eloquent pleas for tolerance ever written in German. It is still performed today, and has been translated into many languages. The character of Nathan himself was clearly modeled on Moses Mendelssohn—a wise, philosophical merchant, setting an example for men of other religions by his own righteous, tolerant, and unselfish way of life. At one point in the play, a Christian monk, realizing at last Nathan's worth, cries out to him: "By God, you are a Christian! There never was a better Christian than you!" Whereupon Nathan the Wise responds, in words which the equally wise Moses Mendelssohn might well have used: "Alas! That which makes me in your eyes a Christian, makes you a Jew in mine."

Commemorative medal struck in honor of Moses Mendelssohn's *Phaedon*. Skull with butterfly over it symbolizes idea of immortality.

Shortly after writing *Nathan the Wise*, Lessing died. He had been ill and weary for many years, and his last letter to Moses was a sad one: "I, too, was a healthy young tree, and now I am a gnarled and rotten trunk. Ah, dear friend, the play is finished. Yet I should have liked to talk to you once more."

Moses Mendelssohn himself died in January 1786, at the age of fifty-six, with his family gathered around him, his fame assured, and his work of helping to lead his people into modern times well begun. The funeral given him by the Jews of Berlin was simple, their grief profound. At the Jewish Free School of Berlin, which he had helped to found, they erected a marble bust with this inscription to him:

WISE AS SOCRATES,
TRUE TO THE FAITH OF HIS FATHERS,
TEACHING, LIKE HIM, IMMORTALITY
AND
BECOMING, LIKE HIM, IMMORTAL.

The Human Hyphen

---⦿---

Abraham Mendelssohn used to tell his friends, with wry humor and also with considerable accuracy, "Formerly I was known as the son of my father, but now I am known as the father of my son." His father, of course, was Moses Mendelssohn, and his son was Felix. If ever a man served as a bridge between two geniuses, it was Abraham Mendelssohn. Once he described himself, self-deprecatingly, as "a human hyphen."

Yet in his own right he was a man of character and breadth of mind. In fact, all of the children of Moses Mendelssohn were remarkable. Two of his three daughters, Henrietta and Recha, pursued careers as educators and preferred intellectual to domestic pursuits. The oldest daughter, Dorothea Mendelssohn, was even more of an original. Adventurous and independent-minded, she became one of the most controversial girls of her time—a forerunner of the Women's Lib movement of today. Dorothea scandalized her contemporaries, including her own family, by leaving her husband to run off with Frederick von Schlegel, a well-known writer considerably younger than herself. Eventually she and Frederick were married, but they continued to lead a tumultuous life, moving from one country to another and undergoing various changes of religion. (Dorothea, who was born Jewish, became both a

Protestant and a Catholic at various times.) Dorothea Mendelssohn wrote a novel as well as several historical works. She also became one of the most renowned hostesses in Europe, conducting a regular salon to which the leading young men and women of the day came to discuss everything from politics to poetry and also to form romantic attachments. Only in her old age did she settle down a bit and turn to such domestic activities as mending and sewing. "There are too many books in the world," she finally concluded, "but I have never heard there are too many shirts."

The three Mendelssohn boys were a good deal more conservative than their sisters. Nathan, Moses Mendelssohn's youngest son, took a university degree in science and spent his life as a successful engineer. The two older sons, Joseph and Abraham, prospered in their banking partnership, with offices in two cities, Hamburg and Berlin.

Abraham was a man with an open and active mind, who liked to investigate new places and ideas. When he decided to learn the financial business, he traveled to Paris to get a job in a French bank called Fould's. As his sister Henrietta was also in Paris, working first as a schoolmistress, then as a governess, he found life there very comfortable. It also was stimulating, for the French Revolution had deposed Louis XVI, and Napoleon Bonaparte was running the country as First Consul. Abraham Mendelssohn found the new political ideals of democracy and equality very much to his liking.

He only returned to Germany because he wished to marry an attractive and highly educated young woman named Leah Salomon, who preferred to live in her own country. So they set up a household first in Hamburg and later in Berlin. They had four children, Fanny, Felix, Rebecca, and Paul, born between 1805 and 1813. Abraham Mendelssohn never gave up his love of travel—which he passed on to his children—but he quickly settled down to the task of being the head of a closely knit family.

Abraham Mendelssohn, the "human hyphen" who was the son of Moses and the father of Felix.

Leah Mendelssohn, mother of Felix. Drawing is by Wilhelm Hensel, artist who married Felix's sister Fanny.

The Mendelssohn children of that era were in a rather enviable position. Materially, the family was well-off—not as wealthy as the Rothschilds, the other great German-Jewish clan, but still plentifully supplied with life's necessities and luxuries alike. The children also had great advantages intellectually and educationally. They were, after all, the grandchildren of the great Moses Mendelssohn, and inherited from him a tradition of love of learning.

Felix's full name was Jacob Ludwig Felix Mendelssohn. He was born on February 3, 1809, while his family was living in Hamburg, where Abraham had charge of the banking office in that city. Much of Felix's time, and that of his sister Fanny, was spent at a pleasant summer home the family owned called Marten's Mill. In later years, when Felix was already famous, Abraham Mendelssohn wrote to Leah: "Dear Wife, we have a certain amount of joy in this young man, and I often think: 'Hurrah for Marten's Mill!' "

An atmosphere of contentment with the progress of all the Mendelssohn children was prevalent in the family from the start, particularly in music. Both parents were excellent musical amateurs and intended to make their children the same. Leah Mendelssohn herself began giving Felix his first piano lessons when he was four years old. She started with instruction periods five minutes long and gradually extended them. For years neither Felix nor Fanny practiced without their mother sitting in the same room, knitting in hand.

As for Abraham, he was never happier than when he saw his children working hard at their music. Like the father of an earlier musical genius, Wolfgang Amadeus Mozart, Abraham realized that he had an extraordinarily talented boy on his hands. And although he did not exploit him commercially, he still wanted him to make the most of his skills.

As befit a self-made man, Abraham was filled with ambition for his children in whatever field they entered. In the Mendelssohn household, the children were awakened at five

Felix Mendelssohn at the piano, a sketch made when he was eleven.

o'clock to begin their morning's lessons. Felix told a friend in later years that he could hardly wait for Sunday to come, so he could sleep later. He said that his father's stern schedule had been "too strenuous" for him. In his childhood he astonished his companions by his ability to fall asleep in an instant. Sometimes he would drop off in midday. It was always a difficult job to rouse him from his slumber. His mother hated to see him idle. Several times, when he was in his room talking to his friend Eduard Devrient, she called out, "Felix, are you doing nothing?" Concluded Devrient: "His brain from childhood had been taxed excessively."

Abraham Mendelssohn engaged a wide variety of tutors for his children. He was determined to spare no expense in educating them. Felix even had his own teacher for landscape painting. Most important of all was his general music instructor, Carl Friedrich Zelter, who was hand-picked by Abraham. Zelter was fifty-nine years old, rough-tongued, and rather coarse in his personal manners. But he was a skilled composer and an able teacher, and he had many musical connections. Among other things, he was director of Berlin's foremost institution for choral music, the Singakademie.

Zelter, it so happened, was a close friend of Johann Wolfgang von Goethe, Germany's foremost literary figure. The seventy-two-year-old "sage of Weimar" not only ruled German letters, but also wielded a strong influence on its science, art, and philosophy. He knew everything and everybody. He had witnessed the entire French Revolution, lived through the rise and fall of Napoleon, helped create the spirit of the new Germany, and written a universal classic in his poetic drama *Faust*.

Goethe's home at Weimar had become almost a shrine. Visitors stood outside reverently, hoping for a glimpse of the old poet strolling in the gardens. To be invited within was considered almost a mystic and ennobling experience.

So highly did Zelter regard Felix that he decided to take his star pupil to meet Goethe and, if possible, spend a few days with him. He wrote to Goethe, describing Felix's unusual abilities and then added, with characteristic crudity: "To be sure, he is the son of a Jew, but no Jew himself. The father, with remarkable self-denial, has let his sons learn something, and educates them properly. It really would be something rare if the son of a Jew turned out to be an artist."

Of course, neither Felix nor his father saw Zelter's letter. It is interesting to speculate on what they might have thought if they had.

In any event, Goethe eagerly invited Zelter and Felix to stay with him at Weimar. It was an unheard-of honor for a twelve-year-old boy.

The visit was an exhilarating experience for Felix. "Now listen, all of you," he wrote to his family on November 10, 1820. "Today is Tuesday. On Sunday the Sun of Weimar—Goethe —arrived. In the morning we went to church and they gave us half of Handel's 100th Psalm. Afterward I went to the Elephant [a hotel] where I sketched the house of Lucas Cranach. Two hours afterwards Professor Zelter came and said, 'Goethe has come; the old gentleman has come,' and in a minute we were down the steps and in Goethe's house. . . . He is very friendly, but I find all his pictures unlike him. . . . One would never take him for seventy-three, but for fifty."

Later that day Felix played for Goethe. He started with Bach and went on to some of his own compositions. Then he improvised. His excitement must have been reflected in his playing, for some of the improvisations were so wild that even Zelter was surprised. "What goblins and dragons are chasing you?" the teacher asked. Felix also played Mozart's *Marriage of Figaro* Overture on the piano for Goethe. The old man immediately began to make the comparisons—by now familiar—between Felix's youthful accomplishments and those of the earlier prodigy.

In the meantime, Felix was receiving by mail all sorts of

instructions from his anxious family as to how to act in Goethe's presence. His father warned him "to sit properly and behave nicely, especially at dinner." His mother wished she could be "a little mouse so as to watch my dear Felix while he is away and see how he comports himself as an independent young man." His sister Fanny told him to keep his eyes and ears open at all times with Goethe and warned that "after you come home, if you can't repeat every word that came from his mouth, I'll have nothing more to do with you."

While on his visit, Felix displayed a precocious interest in other than musical matters. One of the other houseguests was a handsome girl named Ulrike von Pogwisch, the sister of Goethe's daughter-in-law. She took a good deal of interest in Felix's playing, and, for his part, he found her very attractive. "Fräulein Ulrike also threw herself on his [Goethe's] neck," he reported home, "and as he is making love to her, and she is very pretty, it all adds to the general effect."

So pleased was everybody with Felix's visit that Goethe insisted it be prolonged to a total of sixteen days. The poet kept him busy at the piano, playfully remarking to him, "I have not heard you yet today—make a little noise for me." When Felix finally departed, Goethe gave him a generous supply of gifts, including a poem written especially for him. Even more important, Goethe wrote letters to several of his important friends, extolling the young musical marvel from Berlin.

Although his visit with Goethe was the major excursion of Felix's childhood, it was by no means the only long trip he took. When he was seven he journeyed with his family to Paris, where Abraham had financial affairs to look after. While there he took some piano lessons with a famous French pedagogue, Madame Marie Bigot—his first exposure to truly professional musical instruction.

A few years later, the entire household set off on a trip to Switzerland. For Felix this journey almost ended before it

Johann Wolfgang von Goethe, the "sage of Weimar," who invited young Felix to his home and marveled over his achievements as a child prodigy.

began, because he contrived to get himself lost at the first stop, Potsdam. The family was traveling in three carriages, and when they stopped to change horses, Felix dismounted. When the caravan started up again, everybody thought Felix was in another carriage; in reality, he had been busy investigating the stables at Potsdam when the family started out again. Upon discovering that he had been left behind, he started walking down the highway in the direction of the next stop; finally, Abraham's carriage turned back and picked him up.

Felix enjoyed Switzerland immensely. His letters were full of the awe induced by the sight of the great snowy mountains. He also turned a critical ear toward the native music and sent an analysis of Swiss yodeling in a letter he wrote to his music teacher Zelter: "It consists of notes which are produced from the throat and generally are ascending sixths. . . . Certainly this kind of singing sounds harsh and unpleasant when it is heard near by or in a room. But it sounds beautiful when you hear it with mingling or answering echoes, in the valleys, on the mountains, or in the woods. . . ."

For all of young Felix Mendelssohn's precocity, he was anything but a music machine. People who met him as a boy were impressed not merely with his music, but with his good looks, liveliness, and general intelligence. An older boy, Eduard Devrient, who later became Felix's fast friend, first saw him playing marbles outside of his house with other boys. Devrient also remembered seeing him, around the age of thirteen, running along a street with his friends, wearing shoes too large for him and with his brown curls flying.

At eleven Felix entered the Singakademie, singing with the boy altos. He usually sang with his hands thrust in his pockets, swaying from one foot to the other in time to the music. Judging by what Devrient and others said about him, he was one of the most attractive and agreeable, as well as talented, children who ever lived.

Curiously, although he grew up in far different surroundings, there were resemblances between Felix's childhood and that of his grandfather Moses Mendelssohn. Moses seems to have passed along certain physical characteristics to his descendants. Fanny Mendelssohn had a trace of his spinal curvature, and Felix had a slight speech defect, which was described as either a lisp or a drawl. He also bore a strong facial resemblance to his grandfather.

But the principal link between Moses and Felix was their inquisitive spirit. As children, both were bright, precocious, and thirsty for knowledge. But while Moses received his first learning from the local rabbi in Dessau, Felix had access to the latest developments in European art, music, and literature.

It was more than a matter of visiting Goethe or studying with Zelter or traveling to Paris at the age of seven. Felix also learned on his own, and his intellectual interests were just as broad as his grandfather's. He became skilled as a linguist, an artist, and a letter writer. His watercolors are still pleasant to look at and his correspondence a delight to read. He spoke English, French, and Italian, as well as his own German. He studied Latin and Greek. When he was sixteen and a student at the University of Berlin he took as a project a series of translations from the Roman playwright Terence. He liked the results so much that he gave his mother a copy as a birthday present.

Even the childhood entertainment he enjoyed was unusual. He and his sister Fanny, four years his senior, put on a series of Shakespearean performances at home in which the younger children, Rebecca and Paul, also took part. In 1825 the family moved to a new and larger house at 3 Leipzigerstrasse. This was in a remote, almost rural area of Berlin. Their new dwelling was tremendously spacious. In fact, it was an estate covering ten acres in area. It had a vast private park filled with lofty trees, beautiful gardens, a large summer house, and several smaller buildings, plus the luxurious main house itself.

The first summer at 3 Leipzigerstrasse, the Mendelssohn children turned the park into a setting for outdoor Shakespeare. They used a recent translation into German by William August Schlegel, and they went enthusiastically about the business of distributing the parts to themselves and their friends. Their favorite play was *A Midsummer Night's Dream*, and Fanny remembered in later years how they each took turns at all the roles. Indeed, performing under illumination at night amid their stately trees and fragrant lilacs, they might well have applied to themselves the words of Peter Quince in act 3, scene 1: "Pat, pat; and here's a marvelous convenient place for our rehearsal. This green plot shall be our stage, this hawthorne brake our tiring house. . . ."

In one of these summer houses in the park the children also began to publish a "newspaper." They had no printing facilities, so their journal took the form of a stack of blank paper neatly arranged on a table, with several pens and an inkwell near by. Everyone was asked to contribute. At the end of each day, the papers were collected and their contents read aloud. Since the Mendelssohn household attracted a good many distinguished visitors, among the contributors were such famous personages as Alexander Humboldt the explorer, Frederick Hegel the philosopher, and Heinrich Heine the poet. In the summer the journal was called *The Garden Times*, in the winter, *The Tea- and Snow-Times*, or, to use the rather formidable German title, *Thee- und Schneezeitung*.

But all these activities seemed insignificant alongside Felix's tremendous activity as a musician. Ever since those early piano lessons with his mother, he had spent most of his time playing and writing music. In fact, no child since Mozart had composed more prolifically. By the age of eleven he had completed sixty works, ranging from songs and piano pieces to a trio for piano, violin, and cello. At twelve he wrote five string quartets, a motet, and a one-act opera, *The Two School-Teachers*. At thirteen, there were five concertos, six symphonies, and a three-act opera, *The Uncle from Boston*. In 1820 he decided to keep a record of his compositions and began writing them down with the date and place of composition, all in his distinctively neat and precise handwriting. By the end of his life, this list filled forty-four notebooks.

As a performer, too, he started early. He gave his first public concert at the age of nine, appearing with two other musicians. At thirteen he joined a well-known pianist named Aloys Schmitt in a two-piano recital. He didn't receive pay for such appearances, for he was still considered a gifted amateur rather than a professional. Besides, his father, unlike Mozart's father, was wealthy and didn't need to make money from him. At the time there was no thought that Felix would eventually make music his full-time career.

The most important and enjoyable performances Felix gave as a child took place right in his own home. The Mendelssohn family began putting on their own home concerts in their first Berlin residence on the New Promenade, and when they moved to the spacious new quarters at 3 Leipzigerstrasse

Illustration from a Victorian biography depicts Felix as a child directing a home musicale while sister Fanny sits by.

they really expanded them. It was Moses Mendelssohn's open house all over again, though far more elegant and lavish.

Leah Mendelssohn sent out handwritten invitations to musicians and other prominent people, asking them to come to the Mendelssohn musicales, which were held every other Sunday morning. The attractions included luncheon (far more elaborate than Moses' and Fromet's raisins and almonds!) and performances by all the children, for Fanny played the piano, Rebecca sang, and Paul was becoming an expert cellist.

But the big attraction was Felix. Just as travelers to Berlin in the 1770s had been eager to hear old Moses Mendelssohn discourse on philosophy, so were those of the 1820s avid to listen to his grandson Felix make music.

There was nothing haphazard or casual about these performances. Abraham and Leah actually engaged a small orchestra and chorus to come to their house and play. Everything revolved around Felix. He chose the programs, rehearsed the players, and conducted the performances before the invited audience. When he started out, he was so small that he had to stand on a box to be seen by the musicians and the audience alike. Sometimes he also doubled as piano soloist.

Remarkably, none of this adulation and applause turned him into a spoiled child. On the contrary, he worked harder than anybody else concerned. Since many of the works performed were his own compositions, the musical parts had to be copied out for each player. Felix did this work himself, rising at 5:00 A.M. when necessary. Few musicians have become acquainted at such an early age with details of the concert business—not to mention the demands of performing before an audience. And few composers have had the opportunity of finding out so young what their music actually sounded like when played by professional instrumentalists.

At these sessions Felix had a chance to meet some of the foremost musicians of the day, virtually all of whom were fascinated by the amazing young genius. One of these was Ignaz Moscheles, a famous pianist, thirty years old, who was later to become a fast friend of Felix. Leah Mendelssohn wanted him to give her son, then fifteen, some piano lessons, and Moscheles actually had a few sessions with Felix. Finally he turned to Leah and said, "Your son has no need of lessons. If he wishes to take a hint from me as to anything new to him, he can easily do so."

Moscheles was impressed not only by the musical talents of the Mendelssohn group, but by their closeness and warmth as a family. In his diary he wrote: "Felix, a boy of fifteen, is a phenomenon. Compared to him, all other prodigies are only talented children. Both parents are far from overrating their children's talents. In fact, they are worried about Felix's future, and do not know whether he is gifted enough to have a really great career. . . . I told them I was absolutely convinced he would eventually become one of the great masters. . . . I had to keep repeating this over and over before they would believe me."

Moscheles also left a record of two of the programs he heard at the Mendelssohns' home concerts in 1824:

> *Nov. 28, Morning music at the Mendelssohns':*—Felix's C minor Quartet; his D Major Symphony; Concerto by Bach (Fanny); Duet for two pianos in D minor, Arnold.

> *Dec. 12, Sunday music at the Mendelssohns':*—Felix's F minor Quartet. I played my Duet in G for two pianos. Little Schilling played Hummel's Trio in G.

About the same time Professor Zelter, who had been watching his pupil's progress with increasing satisfaction and even awe, wrote to Goethe: "Imagine my joy, if we survive, to see the boy living in the fulfilment of all that his childhood gives promise of." Finally Zelter decided to make some public

recognition of his star pupil. So he arranged a little mock
ceremony after one of the Mendelssohn concerts at which he
called Felix up before him and pronounced before the assembled company, "From this day forth you are no longer an
apprentice but a member of the brotherhood of musicians. I
proclaim you independent, in the name of Mozart, Haydn,
and old father Bach." For all the undercurrent of jesting in
his remarks, Zelter believed in his heart that what he said was
true.

Christian or Jew?

———◦◦◦———

Although Felix's musical progress followed a steady and untroubled course, one other aspect of his childhood was to cause him some uneasy and even agonizing moments—the question of his religion.

By descent, of course, Felix Mendelssohn was Jewish. His grandfather Moses Mendelssohn had been the leading Jew of his generation, and his parents Abraham Mendelssohn and Leah Salomon were both Jewish-born. But for all the improvements in conditions in the years since the death of Moses Mendelssohn, being Jewish still posed grave disabilities. Old Moses, despite his eminence, had never been accepted as an equal by all of his contemporaries. Although there were many Christian Germans like Lessing who wanted to see men of all religions live in perfect brotherhood, there were many others who clung to their ancient prejudices and resisted any change. In discussing Lessing's plays, such as *Nathan the Wise*, one critic wrote that "a noble Jew is a poetic impossibility." Moses Mendelssohn himself, out for a walk with his sons Joseph and Abraham, had once actually been stoned in the street. This was how he described the incident in a letter to a Benedictine monk who was a friend of his:

> Everywhere in this so-called tolerant land, I live so
> isolated through real intolerance, so beset on every

31

side, that, out of love for my own children I lock myself up in a silk factory, as in a cloister. Of an evening I take a walk with my wife and children. "Father," asks one of them innocently, "what are those boys calling us? Why do they throw stones at us? What have we done to them?" "Yes," says another, "they always follow us on the streets and shout 'Jew-boy, Jew-boy!' Is it a disgrace in their eyes to be a Jew? And what does it matter to them?" . . . Ah, I close my eyes, stifle a sigh, and exclaim: "Poor humanity! You have indeed brought things to a sorry pass!"

In Moses' later years he began to witness improvements, at least in the legal status of European Jews, so that he could write: "Blessed be Almighty God who has allowed me, at the end of my days, to see the happy time when the rights of humanity begin to be realized in their true extent." By Abraham's day, Jewish emancipation, set in motion by Moses Mendelssohn, had made much progress. Jews became bankers, businessmen, physicians, and writers, even though many occupations, such as government service and teaching remained closed to them. They could live more or less where they wished and travel in most areas as freely as anyone.

But emancipation also brought about another change—a gradual breakdown of religious traditions. It was a process started inadvertently by Moses Mendelssohn himself, or at least by some of his followers. He had taken the Jews out of the ghetto in an intellectual sense, and now some of them wanted to do likewise in a religious sense. Many Jews, especially those of the upper classes, began to drop their dietary laws and ritual practices. Others went even further and decided to cease being Jews altogether. They accepted conversion to Christianity. Moses Mendelssohn probably would have been horrified at the idea that two of his daughters, Dorothea and Henrietta, were among those who did so.

There were certain advantages to becoming a Christian. It made professional advancement easier and, even more important, brought about social acceptance. Heinrich Heine, the young Jewish poet, said sardonically that conversion was "the admission ticket" to European culture. Heine bought the ticket himself, though ultimately he repented.

Like many other Berlin Jews, Abraham and Leah Mendelssohn faced the question of whether they should undergo conversion. Abraham had prospered in Berlin. In fact, in 1813 he was selected a municipal councillor of the city. So far as religion was concerned, he does not seem to have possessed strong convictions of any kind. There were in all religions, he insisted, "only one God, one virtue, one truth, one happiness."

A letter he wrote to his daughter Fanny, expounding his religious views, has a decidedly modern ring: "Does God exist? What is God? Is He a part of ourselves, and does He continue to live after the other part has ceased to be? And where? And how? All this I do not know, and therefore I have never taught you anything about it. But I know that there exists in me and you and all human beings an everlasting inclination towards all that is good, true, and right, and a conscience which warns and guides us when we go astray. I know it, I believe it, I live in this faith, and this is my religion."

If Abraham Mendelssohn had been left to himself, he probably would have retained his Jewish religion, if only out of respect to the memory of his father. But he wasn't left to himself. Foremost among those urging him to accept conversion was his wife. Leah Mendelssohn was a comely, intelligent, and active woman. She spoke English, French and Italian, and could even read Greek. She was an expert pianist, a good singer, and very interested in art. Many of the Christian intellectuals of the day were among her friends and admirers. She felt she would be even more warmly accepted by them if she were a Christian. Most of all, she thought that being

Jewish was a detriment to her talented children, especially Felix. She felt he would prosper much more readily if he belonged to the prevailing German religion, Lutheranism.

Leah kept urging Abraham at least to permit his children to be baptized as Christians, even if he didn't want to take the step himself. In her discussions with her husband she had the vociferous support of her brother, a rather peculiar personage who bore the name Jacob Bartholdy.

That wasn't the name with which he had been born. His real name was Jacob Levin Salomon, which he despised as being too Jewish sounding. In fact, he didn't like the idea of being Jewish altogether. He cultivated the society of aristocratic and wealthy gentiles, and as a Jew, he felt out of place among them.

So at the age of twenty-four he took the step of becoming a Lutheran and, going even further, also dropped the annoying name of Salomon. He owned a piece of property on the River Spree which had once belonged to a man named Bartholdy. The land and the house on it were still called "Bartholdy's." So Jacob Levin Salomon adopted the name of his property as his own. The new Bartholdy quickly began to lavish money—of which he had plenty—on his new residence. So ornate did he make it that the Mendelssohns made fun of it by calling it "Little Sans Souci," after Frederick the Great's palace. Much to Jacob Bartholdy's chagrin, most other Berliners merely called it "the Jew-Garden."

Bartholdy became a member of the Prussian diplomatic corps and spent many years as consul general in Rome. He lived there on a lavish scale, and his mansion on the Spanish Steps became known for the fine frescoes he commissioned from young painters.

But even though he had money and traveled in exalted circles, few people liked Jacob Bartholdy. Felix Mendelssohn's aunt Henrietta thought him a spendthrift and a wastrel. Nevertheless, he exercised considerable influence over his sister Leah Mendelssohn and, through her, over his broth-er-in-law Abraham.

Leah especially envied him his influential friends. In fact Abraham used to tease her for her "aristocratic inclinations." Bartholdy had a considerable fortune and promised Leah that some day she would inherit it (as she actually did, although it was reduced substantially by his gambling debts). In return he insisted on meddling in the Mendelssohns' affairs. When young Felix began to talk about making music his career, Bartholdy rushed off some advice to the parents: "The idea of a professional musician will not go down with me. It is no career, no life, no aim. . . . Let the boy go through a regular course of schooling, and then prepare for a state career by studying law. . . . Should you prefer him to be a merchant, let him enter a counting-house early."

On matters of religion, Bartholdy was even more persis-tent. His own conversion had been accomplished only after some family unpleasantness. His parents, Babette and Levi Salomon, were opposed to the move. His mother actually cast him out of the family. Only in later years was she reconciled to him.

But Bartholdy never stopped urging Leah and Abraham to become Christians, if not for their own sake then for their children's. He talked to them about it while visiting in Berlin and wrote letters while he was abroad. Leah was willing enough, but Abraham, with the memory of his father on his conscience, was reluctant. Bartholdy kept pestering him, and even proposed that Abraham follow him in altering not only his religion but also his name:

> I was not convinced by your arguments for hold-ing on to your name and faith. Such arguments are no longer valid in our times. . . . You say you owe it to your father's memory, but do you think it would be wrong to give your children the religion

which you regard as the best one? This would be the greatest tribute you or anybody could pay to your father's efforts to spread light and knowledge; in your place he would have done exactly the same for his children, and in my place, perhaps exactly what I have done. You may remain loyal to a despised, persecuted religion and pass it on to your children along with a life of suffering, as long as you believe it to be the absolute truth. But it is barbaric to do so when you no longer so believe.

I urge you to adopt the name Mendelssohn Bartholdy to mark yourself apart from the other Mendelssohns. This would please me very much, because it would be the means of preserving my memory in the family. This would enable you to accomplish your end conveniently, for in France and other places, it is customary to add the name of one's wife's family to one's own.

Between his wife and his brother-in-law, Abraham Mendelssohn was a sorely bedeviled man. Finally he capitulated. In 1816, when Felix was seven years old, he and the rest of the children were marched to the New Church in Berlin where they underwent the rites of baptism and conversion to Christianity.

Their parents, curiously, did not at this time become Christians themselves. Perhaps they feared to offend Leah's formidable mother. But six years later, both Leah and Abraham, finding it difficult to be Jewish parents of Christian children, accepted baptism during a trip to Frankfurt. Henceforth the Mendelssohn family was officially Lutheran, and Abraham added the name Bartholdy to his own.

But the children, though they accepted the changes, kept asking questions about their new name and their new religion. Felix's younger sister Rebecca, who was in some ways the most spunky and sprightly of the lot, for a time refused to be known as Rebecca Mendelssohn Bartholdy. In fact, she signed herself "Rebecca *meden* Bartholdy," *meden* being Greek for "never."

Fanny Mendelssohn also must have given her father a hard time on the subject, for when she underwent confirmation Abraham found it necessary to explain all over again why he had had her accept conversion:

> The outward form of religion your teacher has given you is historical, and changeable like all human ordinances. Some thousands of years ago the Jewish form was the reigning one, then the heathen form, and now it is the Christian. We, your mother and I, were born and brought up by our parents as Jews, and without being obliged to change the form of our religion have been able to follow the divine instinct in us and in our conscience. We have educated you and your brothers and sister in the Christian faith, because it is the creed of most civilized people, and contains nothing that can lead you away from what is good, and much that guides you to love, obedience, tolerance and resignation, even if it offered nothing but the example of its Founder, understood by so few, and followed by still fewer.

Felix proved even more difficult to handle. In fact, the question of whether Felix Mendelssohn was a "Jewish composer" not only was raised in his lifetime, but has continued to plague critics and biographers right down to the present.

He certainly was not a Jewish composer in the sense that he wrote "Jewish music." Attempts have been made to find echoes of synagogue chants or Hebraic cantillations in his music; but none are very convincing. But in his personal life, although he retained his adherence to Lutheranism to the end, there were marked Jewish influences and interests.

As a boy, he had several overt encounters with anti-Semitism, just as his grandfather Moses had. In 1819 Prussia was swept by a series of anti-Jewish demonstrations. While they were going on, Felix happened to meet in the street a Prussian royal prince with whom he had a slight acquaintance. The boy marched up to him, spat at his feet, called him a "Jewboy" and ran off. A few years later he and Fanny, vacationing with their family at the shore, ran into a gang of toughs who called them similar names.

Such incidents seemed to strengthen Felix's feelings for his Jewish origins. He had the deepest respect for his father's opinions, but he also had a strong streak of stubbornness in his character. So a conflict within him over the Jewish question was inevitable. It came out openly when he was sixteen years old. His father was on a business trip to Paris, and he took Felix along, planning to introduce him to some musical personalities in the French capital. Since his son was about to step out into the world, Abraham engraved some calling cards for him. They bore the name "Felix M. Bartholdy." Felix refused to accept them. His name, he said, was not Bartholdy but Mendelssohn, although out of respect to his father he would agree to be called Felix Mendelssohn Bartholdy.

Again and again during their ride in a jolting carriage Felix asked his father why he had changed his name. Abraham, distressed at the question, attempted to justify his action by pointing out that Moses Mendelssohn, too, had changed his name from Moses Dessau.

"This small change was decisive," argued Abraham. "As Mendelssohn, he detached himself from an entire class, the best of whom he raised to his own level. By that name he identified himself with a different group."

Felix was unconvinced, and finally Abraham gave up the attempt to make him use the "Bartholdy" cards. Four years later the quarrel was renewed. Felix was then on his first visit to London, appearing as a conductor and composer. His name was featured on placards and printed in programs—always as "Felix Mendelssohn." He sent one of the programs and several newspaper clippings back to Abraham, who was incensed. "I am greatly dissatisfied about this," his father wrote to him. "You have committed a great wrong. A name may be only a name, but as long as you are under your father's guardianship, you have the clear and undeniable duty to be known by his name. . . . You cannot, you must not carry the name Mendelssohn. Felix Mendelssohn Bartholdy is too long; it is unsuited for daily use. You must go by the name Felix Bartholdy."

As a clinching argument, Abraham attempted to convince Felix that to use the name Mendelssohn was almost an insult to old Moses, who had made it famous in Jewry. "A Christian Mendelssohn is an impossibility," he argued. "There can no more be a Christian Mendelssohn than a Jewish Confucius. If Mendelssohn is your name, you are *ipso facto* a Jew."

But Felix, who yielded to his father in so many matters, was adamant on this one. He retained the name Mendelssohn to the end of his life.

The Young Composer

When Felix was in his teens he began to consider seriously the question of his future. Or rather, his family did. Felix himself never had any doubt but that he wanted to be a musician—both a performer and a conductor. But Abraham and Leah weren't so sure. Their son had been a musical marvel from the start, but they knew that musical history was studded with the cases of prodigies who burned themselves out and never lived up to their youthful promise. They also knew that many able musicians, Berliners and others, had pronounced Felix a genuine genius rather than a merely talented youth. But Berlin, after all, was then a provincial capital, not a world center like Paris or London. Over and over again, family councils were held to discuss whether and when to expose Felix to the judgment of musicians in foreign cities.

Abraham's trip to Paris in 1825 afforded the perfect chance. He planned to spend some time in the city, so Felix would have an opportunity to attend the opera and the symphony, as well as to mingle with French musical leaders, most of whom were already acquainted, at least by reputation, with the talents of the Berlin banker's son.

Foremost among those whom Felix wanted to meet was Luigi Cherubini, the Italian-born director of the Paris Conservatory. Cherubini, sixty-five, was the monarch of French music, and he spoke with an imperious tongue. Felix called him "an extinct volcano." Abraham engaged three string players to participate with Felix in a performance of a newly written piano quartet. Cherubini was impressed. "This boy is rich," he pronounced at the end. "He will do well. He is already doing well."

This verdict was the most pleasant thing that happened to Felix in Paris because, as it turned out, he did not care for the city very much. Parisians were too frivolous and flighty for his taste. Especially in music he found himself in sharp disagreement with the prevalent fashions. People liked only "trivial, showy music," he complained in a letter to Fanny. She wrote back advising him to play Bach and Beethoven for the Parisians, to show them what good music was really like. "That is just what I am trying to do," he replied. "But remember, my dear child, that these people do not know a single note of [Beethoven's opera] *Fidelio*, and regard Bach as a mere old-fashioned wig stuffed with learning."

One day, when Felix had been praising Bach, a Parisian musician asked him to play some of his works. Felix chose two organ preludes in E minor and B minor, which he regarded as powerful examples of Bach's art. The audience listened politely and then one of them remarked, "The A minor's opening is very much like a duet in Monsigny, don't you think?" Felix emphatically didn't think, and said so. Monsigny was a composer of pleasant, though trifling tunes. "Everything danced before my eyes," Felix wrote Fanny, in reporting his reaction to the incident. His letters were filled with savage comments on many of the foremost figures of the day, for he combined musical insight with youthful impudence. For example, of Franz Liszt, just beginning his career as the most fashionable pianist of the day, the sixteen-year-old Felix wrote crisply: "Liszt plays very well; he has many fingers, but few brains."

Bach, Beethoven, and Mozart were Felix's musical idols in

his young days, and they remained so throughout his life. That seems natural enough today, when all three of these composers are enshrined on the topmost level of the musical pantheon. But in Mendelssohn's day, Bach was widely neglected so far as actual performances went, and Mozart was usually presented in a prettified style and with extraneous embellishments added to his music. As for Beethoven, who died in 1827, when Felix was eighteen years old, he was the bane of the older, more conservative generation. In fact, Beethoven, like religion, was a point of contention between Felix and his father. Abraham Mendelssohn especially regarded the later Beethoven works, such as the Ninth Symphony, the "Hammerklavier" Sonata, and the final string quartets, as incomprehensible. The aged Goethe reacted similarly when Felix played him a piano version of Beethoven's Fifth Symphony. The poet said it sounded "as if the house were caving in." Nevertheless, Felix played Beethoven wherever he went. He even memorized a piano reduction of the Ninth Symphony, as well as the "Hammerklavier." It was a great source of regret to him that he never met Beethoven.

Beethoven symbolized something more than a composer of originality and power to Felix. He also represented the blending of two great musical traditions, the classical and the romantic. He was the bridge from one to the other, because it was through Beethoven that music became a personal vehicle of expression, a statement of a composer's credo as well as an exercise of his intellect. Perhaps more than any composer of his time, Felix Mendelssohn felt the pull of both the old world and the new. That is why he became known as a "romantic classicist" or a "classical romantic"—either term is accurate.

Mendelssohn's early compositions—those he began in childhood and continued through his mid-teens—were for the most part smooth and well-constructed works that showed his technical skill. But gradually signs of originality appeared. The young composer was beginning to assert his identity. He even started a strange practice that he continued throughout his life: at the top of each composition, as he finished it, he wrote the cryptic letters *L.e.g.G.* or *H.d.m.* He never told anybody what they meant. As possible explanations, commentators have suggested the German words *Lobt einen guten Gott* ("Praise a Good God") and *Hilf du mir* ("Help Thou Me"). But these are only guesses, and the mystery remains unsolved to this day.

Musically Mendelssohn also began a practice that remained uniquely his own to the end of his life. He started to compose a series of scherzos such as had never been heard in music before. The word *scherzo* means "joke" and signifies a sprightly, humorous movement in a musical work. It had been none other than Mendelssohn's idol Beethoven who had begun to write scherzos for the third movements of his symphonies and quartets, in place of the old-fashioned, more formal minuets. Felix followed suit. But his scherzos were different. They had an elfin, enchanted, imaginative quality that set them apart from anything ever written by Beethoven, or any one else. One of the first of these was the light and graceful scherzo of the piano quartet (in B minor) which Felix had played for Cherubini in Paris. He must have thought this work something special, for he later dedicated it to his friend Goethe.

In 1825 Felix took what one critic called "a wonderful leap into maturity." He composed, for performance at the Sunday musicales, a composition for two first violins, two second violins, two violas, and two cellos, which remains his first enduring masterpiece. This Octet in E-flat, opus 20, is music of such radiance and vitality that it remains an incredible achievement for a boy of sixteen. Not even Mozart wrote anything like it at that age. And of course it has a scherzo, a wonderfully light-fingered, gossamer movement that never fails to enchant a listener no matter how often he hears it. Felix talked the movement over with his sister Fanny, and later she wrote this account of it: "To me alone he told his idea: the whole piece is to be played staccato and pianissimo, the tremolandos coming in now and then, the trills passing away with the quickness of lightning; everything new and strange and at the same time most insinuating and pleasing. One feels so near the world of spirits, carried away in the air, half inclined to snatch up a broomstick and follow the aerial procession. At the end the first violin takes flight with a feathery lightness—and all has vanished." Felix himself said years later that the Octet remained his favorite work and added, "I had a beautiful time writing it."

It was no accident that Felix discussed his scherzo in advance with Fanny, for between brother and sister there existed a bond of love and mutual respect. All the Mendelssohn children got along with each other with remarkable amiability. If there were ever quarrels between them, they probably did not last long, for there is no record of them.

Felix's younger sister Rebecca was a sprightly, pretty girl with a good singing voice and an impish sense of humor. Once Felix decided to study Greek, but didn't want to take lessons alone, so Rebecca obligingly went along with him. On another occasion she came down with measles, and Felix was so upset that he postponed a trip he was scheduled to take. A few days later he caught the disease too and, according to his own account, was very happy about it because now they could spend their convalescence together. Rebecca, like all the Mendelssohns, was aware that she had a genius as a brother, but she showed no resentment. She was never happier than when she was singing Felix's songs at the family musicales.

Paul, the youngest child, was, as it turned out, the least musical, although he learned to play the cello well enough for Felix to compose several pieces for him. From the start Paul was the solid citizen of the family, destined to go into the banking business and later on looking after the financial affairs of the rest of the Mendelssohns, including Felix.

Fanny (right) and Rebecca Mendelssohn, sisters of Felix, as drawn by Wilhelm Hensel.

But it was Fanny and Felix who were an inseparable pair. Although she was four years older, they treated each other as absolute equals. Like him, she was a superb pianist—in fact, when people praised Felix for his playing, he would often answer, "But you should hear my sister Fanny!" When Fanny was thirteen years old she gave her father a present no other girl would have thought of: she played him twenty-four Bach preludes by heart.

Fanny was also a composer. She wrote piano pieces, songs, and a lovely Trio for Piano and Strings. She and Felix used to take turns at playing each other's works. He jokingly called her "the Cantor," and imitated her habit of making little coughing noises when she disliked something he had written. "They are really vain and proud of each other," their mother remarked.

But Abraham Mendelssohn, who was so liberal in other matters, strongly disapproved of the idea of a girl appearing in public as a musical performer, or even of publishing her compositions. So Fanny was deprived of a chance to make her talents known anywhere except at the family's Sunday musicales. As if to compensate, she devoted herself wholeheartedly to the furtherance of Felix's career, and he showed her almost every note as he wrote it. When she was seventeen and Felix thirteen, Fanny proudly wrote: "I have watched his progress step by step, and may say I have contributed to his development. I have always been his only musical adviser, and he never writes down a thought before submitting it to my judgment. I have known his operas by heart before a note was written."

When Felix was seventeen, he showed Fanny a new composition, the finest achievement of his career so far, and perhaps as fine as anything he ever composed later. It was an Overture to *The Midsummer Night's Dream*, the play that the children had performed in their garden. Listening in her mind to the four woodwind chords that begin the work, and that seem to open up a whole moonlit universe, Fanny realized that her brother had composed a full-fledged masterpiece.

So did most other people who heard it for the first time. The *Midsummer Night's Dream* Overture created a sensation when it was performed at a Sunday musicale in the garden house at 3 Leipzigerstrasse. Soon invitations began arriving for the young composer to conduct it elsewhere. Its first public performance was in the city of Stettin on February 20, 1827. Felix also made a version of it for two pianos, for himself and Fanny to play together.

So widely discussed was the Overture that all sorts of stories sprang up about it. According to one account, Felix dashed it off at the piano while sitting beside a young neighbor girl he was fond of. Another story said he composed it at a little table in the family garden while the evening breezes wafted past him, each bringing to him one of the opening chords. Still a third version was that he surreptitiously wrote it out on music paper while attending a dull lecture at the University of Berlin.

The important thing was that almost everybody who heard it recognized that Mendelssohn had introduced a new strain into music, depicting the world of the imagination as no one else ever had. One contemporary critic remarked with prescience: "Here begins a new music."

Not everything was such a success for young Felix. He tried to write an opera, and failed. In fact, he failed so badly that he never again made a serious attempt to compose opera, although he always kept looking for a suitable subject.

Several of his childhood operas had been produced informally at the Mendelssohn musicales. But at sixteen Felix made a really ambitious attempt by composing a three-act comedy entitled *The Wedding of Camacho*. It was based on an episode in Cervantes' *Don Quixote*. One of the characters in the opera was the Don himself. The plot itself was far from inspired—all about the rivalry of a rich landowner and a poor peasant lad for the hand of a pretty girl—although many successful operas have been built on less.

Felix thought his opera was good enough to be produced at the Royal Theater of Berlin, which was directed by Gasparo Spontini, a celebrated Italian operatic composer. Spontini was well acquainted with the Mendelssohn family, but he was in no hurry to produce Felix's opera. After delaying nearly a year, he finally give his consent and *The Wedding of Camacho* went on the stage. A distinguished audience was present, among them the Sunday afternoon "regulars" from the family musicales. A few were old friends going back to the era of Moses Mendelssohn.

But despite the presence of a sympathetic audience, the

opera somehow failed to make its effect. People began to drift out—and not return. The applause diminished with each act. Even Felix, listening restlessly in the wings, realized that his music, which had looked so good on paper, simply wasn't sounding as good in actual performance. He felt a sinking sensation inside him, and he decided to slip out of the stage door just as the performance ended. In that way he didn't have to face his friends and family until later. It wasn't a very courageous exit, perhaps, but one that was understandable in a boy of seventeen.

Felix had several other experiences with adverse criticism, for the novelty of some of his music sometimes disturbed the older generation. Usually he would brush off such critics, but once he was stirred to write a poem in reply:

> *If the artist gravely writes,*
> *To sleep it will beguile.*
> *If the artist gaily writes,*
> *It is a vulgar style.*
>
> *If the artist writes at length,*
> *How sad his hearer's lot!*
> *If the artist briefly writes,*
> *No man will care one jot.*
>
> *If an artist simply writes,*
> *A fool he's said to be,*
> *If an artist deeply writes,*
> *He's mad, 'tis plain to see.*
>
> *In whatsoever way he writes*
> *He can't please every man;*
> *Therefore let an artist write*
> *How he likes and can.*

The failure of *Camacho* upset Mendelssohn for a time. But he had too much music in his head and vigor in his heart to remain depressed for long. A summer trip to the Harz Mountains with two young friends, Eduard Rietz, a violinist, and Gustav Magnus, a physician, restored his spirits. After one particularly exhilarating excursion near the town of Erbich ("a poor little place"), he wrote home:

> If three of the most remarkable families of Berlin knew that three of their most remarkable sons are roving the roads at night with carriers, peasants and tramps, and exchanging biographies with them, they would be dreadfully distracted. . . . In all the towns, hamlets and villages we go through with our pilgrim-staffs we cause great excitement; the girls come to the windows, and the street-boys follow us laughing for three streets at the least—a proof of popularity and clean linen! We get on together quite well as we enjoy ourselves, and this is saying a great deal. Our talk is alternately of musicians, fevers, and home, so each has his own topic, and in a student song and refrain we all join as one. . . .

One consequence of the triumph of the *Midsummer Night's Dream* Overture was a parting of the ways, as pupil and teacher, of Mendelssohn and his old tutor Zelter. Although it was not put into so many words, the feeling in the family now was that Felix had outgrown the crusty old pedagogue and could operate musically entirely on his own. Zelter remained on more or less friendly terms with the family and, as a matter of fact, spent the remaining eight years of his life taking bows for Felix's achievements. "The old man has seen the fish swim," commented one of Felix's friends, "and imagines he has taught him how."

The Great Bach Revival

Although Zelter no longer was Felix's teacher, he now was to play an important part in one of the most momentous events of his life—his rescue from a century of neglect of a musical masterpiece by Johann Sebastian Bach.

Today it seems incredible to us that a work like Bach's *Passion According to St. Matthew* should have gone unperformed for a hundred years. Bach had composed it in 1729 for his own church in Leipzig—a dramatic and beautiful musical reenactment of the story of the judgment and crucifixion of Jesus. Although it made a deep impression on its first listeners, it had never been repeated. Musicians knew of the existence of this great choral masterpiece, but nobody ever performed it, and it had never been printed. The general public had never had a chance to hear it.

As 1829, the hundredth anniversary of the *St. Matthew Passion* approached, Felix determined to restore it to life. He knew that Zelter, as the director of Berlin's foremost choral singing society, the Singakademie, possessed a copy of the score, copied by hand from Bach's original. He talked about it to the family, expressing a desire to examine Zelter's score, with the idea of performing a few of the choruses at one of the Sunday musicales.

Felix's grandmother, old Madame Salomon, hearing of his

interest, decided to go him one better. She engaged a copyist to make a copy of the *St. Matthew* score in the Singakademie library and presented it to Felix as a Christmas gift.

Felix was ecstatic. All through that winter he and his musical friends tried out parts of the *Passion* in the Mendelssohn home. Soon a small choir was assembled to sing the chorales. The results were overwhelming. Everyone who participated even in those fragmentary performances was struck by the grandeur of the music. Felix almost immediately began dreaming of a public performance of the *Passion*.

Felix had a strong ally in his friend Eduard Devrient, a young actor. Devrient, it may be remembered, had known Felix since he was a child playing marbles outside his home; he was older than Felix, but he had the utmost respect for his abilities and regarded him as a leader. Although Eduard was heading for an acting career, he was the possessor of a sturdy bass voice and knew how to sing. The role of Jesus in the *St. Matthew Passion* is written for a bass or a baritone, and Eduard wanted to sing it in a complete performance conducted by Felix.

Felix was willing enough. But he knew there was only one place the massive and difficult *Passion* could be given—at the Singakademie itself, with the full participation of the large chorus of that institution. Naturally, this depended on the cooperation of Zelter, and Felix went to talk to him at his office.

He found his old teacher surprisingly reluctant to get involved in the project. Zelter told Felix that the music was difficult to perform, that it would require numerous rehearsals, that hundreds of people would have to participate—all of which Felix knew. Zelter also knew a few other things that hadn't occurred to the eager young man. He knew that there were some members of the Singakademie, which consisted of the most aristocratic families of Berlin, who didn't exactly approve of the young Jewish-born composer. Many of them regarded the Mendelssohns as upstarts who had no business in an organization like the Singakademie to begin with. Whatever his reasons, Zelter rebuffed Felix's first attempts to perform the *St. Matthew Passion.*

But Eduard Devrient, himself a member of the Singakademie, was determined not to give up. One night in January 1829, after singing at a practice session devoted to the *Passion,* he resolved to urge Felix to make another effort to win over his old teacher. The next morning Devrient arrived at the Mendelssohn house just after the late winter dawn had broken. Felix was still asleep, but his brother Paul, then sixteen, eagerly volunteered to awaken him. This was no easy matter, for Felix was well known for the depth of his slumber.

Paul slipped his arms under his inert brother and propped him up against the pillow. "Felix, wake up, it's eight o'clock," he shouted. Felix slept on, and Paul began rocking his body back and forth while Devrient looked on fascinated. Felix, who apparently was dreaming of music, muttered, "Oh, stop it, I always said so, it's sheer squawking." Finally he opened his eyes and, seeing Devrient standing grinning by his bed, exclaimed, "Hey, Eduard, what are you doing here?" Devrient told him he had something to talk to him about. Then the three young men went into Felix's study, where coffee was percolating on a stove, and had breakfast.

While they ate, Devrient told Mendelssohn that he wanted him to make one more try with Zelter. His plan was for Felix to conduct, himself to sing Jesus, and Zelter to give them the use of the concert hall. He suggested that they propose to Zelter that the proceeds go to charity, thus making it difficult for the Singakademie board of trustees to refuse. Moreover, he suggested that they go see Zelter immediately—that very morning.

"All right," said Felix, "but I will leave if Zelter gets nasty and begins to quarrel."

"He'll certainly get nasty," replied Devrient, "but leave the quarreling to me."

At the Singakademie, they went into Zelter's office. Remembered Devrient: "We found the old giant sitting at his grand piano with its double keyboards, a long pipe in his mouth, and a dense cloud of tobacco smoke surrounding him. . . . He was wearing his usual short, snuff-colored, beribboned and betasseled Polish jacket and knee breeches, stockings of coarse wool and embroidered shoes. . . . He peered at us through his spectacles, and when he saw who it was he called out good-naturedly: 'What do two such handsome lads want with me so early in the day? To what am I indebted for this honor? Here, sit down. . . .' "

Devrient then launched into his well-studied speech about how they admired Sebastian Bach, dreamed about performing his *Passion*, had already begun working on it, and now wished his permission to use the Akademie for this noble purpose.

Zelter listened gloomily and replied, "Oh yes, that is all very well, but nowadays things like that can't be done so easily." He enumerated the obstacles: the need for extra musicians, the difficulties of the music, the inadequacies of the choristers, problems, problems. . . . Mendelssohn, who had heard it all before, edged toward the door, but Devrient persisted. He told Zelter that under his wise guidance the Singakademie chorus had reached such a pinnacle of excellence that it could meet the challenge, and that the orchestra, too, would rise to the occasion. Zelter replied impatiently that "much better people than you two" had talked of putting on the *Passion* and never done so. "Why should a couple of snotnoses like you succeed?" he asked with characteristic crudity.

Mendelssohn was standing with his hand on the doorknob by now, but Devrient kept arguing: "We may be young but we're not so immature. After all, young people are supposed to have a certain amount of courage and enterprise, and a teacher should be pleased if two of his pupils want to attempt something so important." Zelter answered that the women on the board of trustees would oppose the plan, but Devrient told him that some had actually joined in the choral rehearsals at the Mendelssohn home. "Women!" Zelter exclaimed scornfully. "Today ten of them come to rehearsals and tomorrow twenty stay away!"

The two young men dutifully laughed at the joke and went right on arguing. Finally Zelter began to weaken and promised at least to lay the question before the board of trustees. "I won't oppose you," he said, "and will put in a good word for you if I can." His last words before he ushered them out of the door were: "Good luck to you, and we'll see what comes of it all."

Devrient and Mendelssohn rushed out into the street exulting and shaking hands with each other. "To think," Felix exclaimed, "that an actor and a Jew should give back to the people the greatest Christian music in the world." It was the only time, Devrient later wrote, that Mendelssohn ever mentioned in his hearing his Jewish origin.

As Zelter had predicted, there was considerable grumbling within the Singakademie over the proposed performance. Felix made a point of calling personally on some of the trustees to explain what he wanted to do. He even purchased a pair of yellow kid gloves before going, just to make sure he was dressed in the proper fashion for such a formal undertaking. Finally the trustees agreed to permit the hall to be used for the purpose, but, charity affair or not, they refused to waive the customary fifty-thaler fee for its rental. So Felix dug down into his own pocket and came up with the money.

Fortunately, everybody else connected with the project was much more cooperative. Most of the solo singers, drawn from the Berlin Opera, refused compensation and even offered to pay their way in to the concert. None of them, it should be remembered, had ever seen the music before, and all had to learn it from scratch. In the end, only six free tickets were issued for the concert, and two of these went to the opera director, Spontini, who disapproved of the whole business.

As rehearsals were going on for the big event, word began to spread through Berlin musical circles of the magnificence and splendor of the music. The result was that the concert, on March 11, 1829, was sold out weeks in advance, and on the night of the performance more than a thousand people were turned away at the door.

The twenty-year-old Felix, facing the greatest audience he had ever seen and the largest array of performers he had ever conducted, directed the performance masterfully. His sister Fanny sang in the chorus with the altos. Wrote Fanny afterward in a letter to a friend: "I sat at the corner, where I could see Felix very well. . . . The choruses were sung with a fire, a striking power, and also with a touching delicacy and softness such as I have never heard. . . . The room had the air of a church: the deepest quiet and most solemn devotion pervaded the whole, only now and then involuntary utterances of intense emotion were heard."

The public reception to Bach's masterpiece was overwhelming. Having been deprived of it so long, music lovers responded with instant acclaim. A second performance had to be scheduled for the Singakademie ten days after the first. This time extra seats were put up in the lobby and in a small rehearsal hall that opened onto the main hall, with the doors left open so that all might hear it. Thus the crowd at the second hearing was even larger than at the first, and once again the ovation seemed endless. Afterward, Zelter invited all the principal participants to his home for a celebration. With Felix seated at the head of the table, the conviviality and congratulations lasted far into the night.

Mendelssohn's revival of the *St. Matthew Passion* in Berlin was followed by performances of the work in other cities. The music publishing house of Schlesinger printed the score, in a piano reduction. Everywhere people were talking about the great music Felix Mendelssohn had rescued from obscurity. Interest begin to grow in other music by old Bach which, like his *Passion,* had lain in obscurity for a century. Undoubtedly

Bach's greatness was bound to have been rediscovered by someone along the line, for he was too important a master to have been forgotten forever. But it is a matter of historical record that today's universal understanding and appreciation of Johann Sebastian Bach began with the revival of the *St. Matthew Passion* in 1829 by twenty-year-old Felix Mendelssohn.

The Conquest of London

The Mendelssohn family loved to travel. In an era when journeying from one country, or even one city, to another was an arduous and even dangerous process, they managed to make visits to France and Switzerland, as well as to move about in their own country.

Now that Felix was twenty years old, it was decided at a family council that the time had come for him to see a bit of the world on his own. There were several reasons for him to leave Berlin. After his triumph in the *St. Matthew Passion* the city seemed to have little to offer in the way of musical advancement. Besides, Felix was never completely happy in Berlin. He always felt an undercurrent of resentment from some of the city's social and artistic leaders. There were people who held against him that he was wealthy and Jewish and had never really had to earn his own way. Some people even deprecated his abilities. Henry F. Chorley, an English music critic visiting Prussia, reported hearing Berliners say of the youthful Felix, "Mendelssohn? Ah, he had talent as a boy." Obviously there was little to be lost by spending a few years visiting other European lands.

So Felix and his father put their heads together and mapped out an itinerary. For the next three years he would pursue a series of journeys that would take him across the Continent,

57

to London, Paris, Vienna, Rome, and other cities. From time to time his crisscross path would bring him home for brief stopovers in Berlin. When he found a city or country that interested him particularly, he would remain there for an indefinite stay. His was to be a Grand Tour in the grandest sense. And his first stop would be London, a city that he had never visited.

Perhaps we should pause for a moment to consider what life was like at this time in England, because it was to become Felix Mendelssohn's second home. He visited Britain ten times in his short lifetime and was regarded there for years as almost its national composer. England then was on the verge of the Victorian age, although Queen Victoria herself did not ascend the throne until eight years later, in 1837. London was the capital of a vast industrial and commercial power beginning its climb toward the zenith. The Industrial Revolution was centered in England. Everywhere were factories, railways, bustling business establishments. By comparison Berlin seemed a poky, hidebound, provincial capital.

In music, too, London far outdazzled Berlin in the variety and vitality of its enterprises. The Philharmonic Society, founded in 1813, led a flourishing life. Opera abounded, with large audiences coming out to applaud top singers from all over Europe.

The one thing the British lacked was composers of their own. Not since Henry Purcell's death in 1695 had England produced a creative musical genius. By way of compensation, the British adopted certain great foreign composers as their own. George Frideric Handel settled in London in 1712 and dominated its musical life until his death in 1759. Joseph Haydn made two extended visits in the 1790s, writing his greatest symphonies there and being lionized by the London public. The last of this triumvirate of German-speaking composers was to be Felix Mendelssohn, who left an imprint on British musical life that persisted for nearly a century.

To send Felix off to England with a proper show of family affection, his father and his younger sister Rebecca accompanied him to Hamburg, where he boarded a steamer called the *Attwood*. Steam was then a fairly recent development in sea transport, and the *Attwood*'s engine kept breaking down in heavy seas. Felix had recently written an overture called *Calm Sea and Prosperous Voyage,* and he repented it bitterly during the three days of the crossing, for he was seasick almost the entire time.

He was met at the dock by two friends, Ignaz Moscheles, the pianist who had once given him lessons and was now a resident of London, and Karl Klingemann, a young German diplomat from Hanover whom he had known in Berlin. They had found him lodgings with a German iron dealer at 103 Great Portland Street, at the corner of Ridinghouse Street.

On his very first day, Klingemann took Felix to a London coffeehouse where he read in the *Times*—his English was fluent—that the famous singer Maria Malibran was performing in Rossini's opera *Otello* at the King's Theater that night. Felix forthwith bought a ticket and went to hear her. Malibran was one of the most exciting singers of the day, and Felix was duly impressed. He wrote home that he had found her "a young woman, beautiful and splendidly made, her hair *en toupet,* full of fire and power, very coquettish. . . . I shall go constantly to hear her." His introduction to English musical life also impressed him because of the endurance of the audience. It was not until nearly 1:00 A.M. that Malibran, in the role of Desdemona, was finally smothered by her Othello. Felix, still exhausted from his channel crossing, went home —although another work, a ballet, remained to be given on the program.

Mendelssohn was fascinated by London from the moment he got there. In his letters home he could hardly contain his exuberance and delight:

No. 3 Chester Place, London—a drawing made by Mendelssohn.
His friend Moscheles lived in the house.

London is the grandest and most complicated mon-
ster on the face of the earth. . . . Not in the last six
months at Berlin have I seen so many contrasts and
such variety as in these last three days. Could you
but once, turning to the right from my lodging,
walk down Regent Street and see the wide bright
street with its arches (alas! it is enveloped in a thick
fog today!). . . . There are beggars, Negroes, and
those fat John Bulls with their slender, beautiful
daughters in pairs on their arms. Ah, those daughters! . . . Last but not least, to see the masts from the
West India docks stretching their heads over the
housetops, and to see a harbor as big as the Hamburg one treated like a mere pond, with sluices, and
the ships arranged not singly but in rows, like regi-
ments—to see all that makes one's heart rejoice at
the greatness of the world.

Under the tutelage of Klingemann and Moscheles, Mendelssohn quickly got into the London swing. He went to an
English tailor and ordered a complete new outfit in the London mode. He had himself painted by a fashionable artist,
James Warren Childe, wearing his elegant new clothes, including top hat, and looking for all the world like an English
dandy. He went to diplomatic receptions with Klingemann
and to musical soirees with Moscheles. He quickly became
known as one of the most fascinating young men in London.
For his part, he developed an eye for the English girls, whom
he found unusually attractive.

Girls had always interested Felix, starting with his own
sisters. In one of his first letters from London he reported to
the family that he had been seated alongside "two very wonderful brown eyes" at a dinner party. Another time he went
to a phrenology exhibition at which a "doctor" examined the
bumps on a pretty girl's head. After watching the girl undo

Felix Mendelssohn as an English dandy. This watercolor was made in 1829 during his first visit to England at the age of twenty.

her long hair so the doctor could feel the contours of her skull, Felix reported: "I gave three cheers for phrenology and praised everything concerned with it."

Felix also liked English cookery, which is not usually rated very high on the international gastronomy scale. He sent home redolent descriptions of plum pudding and cherry pie, "German sausages" that one could purchase from street vendors, and a succulent dish of crabs consumed on a visit to the seacoast resort of Ramsgate.

Mendelssohn also went the rounds of the London art galleries and visited the theaters. He was dismayed by a performance he saw of *Hamlet* with the famous actor Kemble in the leading part. Felix, who knew his Shakespeare, was shocked to find passages omitted and scenes abridged, including the instructions of Polonius to Laertes, and one of Hamlet's soliloquies. Kemble, he reported, shouted at the top of his voice and played Hamlet with one yellow and one black leg to indicate his madness. Worst of all, at the very end, after Hamlet said "The rest is silence" and sank dead to the floor, Horatio left his side, advanced to the footlights, and announced to the audience: "Ladies and gentlemen, tomorrow evening *The Devil's Elixir.*" Commented Mendelssohn in his report to the family: "I believe, children, that he was right who said that the English sometimes do not understand Shakespeare."

He found, however, that they understood music very well. To an extent, his reputation as a young composer and conductor had preceded him. The "Diary of a Dilettante" column in a musical publication called *Harmonicum* reported: "Another arrival in London is the young M. Mendelssohn, son of the rich banker of Berlin, and I believe, grandson of the celebrated Jewish philosopher and elegant writer. He is one of the finest piano-forte players in London, and is supposed to be better acquainted with music than most professors of the art."

His formal debut in London came when the city's most

prestigious orchestra, the Philharmonic Society, invited him to conduct a concert on May 25, 1829, at the Argyll Rooms on Regent Street. Felix played one of his works, the Symphony no. 1 in C minor, composed five years earlier. For the occasion he decided to scrap the symphony's original third movement, a minuet, and substitute for it the quicksilvery scherzo from his Octet, which he orchestrated. The entire symphony delighted the audience, and the scherzo was such a hit that he had to play it a second time. Five days later Felix appeared as a piano soloist with the Philharmonic, playing the *Concertstück* by Carl Maria von Weber. At this concert, he arrived at the hall early to try out the piano, and became so absorbed in his playing that he didn't notice the audience had begun to arrive and was listening appreciatively to the unexpected performance. Shortly afterward Felix played Beethoven's "Emperor" Concerto with the Philharmonic, and also conducted his *Midsummer Night's Dream* Overture, which won him a tremendous ovation.

Within a few weeks, Felix had conquered London as composer, conductor, and pianist. It is almost impossible to overstate the impact that the twenty-year-old youth made on the sophisticated city. One modern parallel might be the sensation created overnight in New York in 1943, when Leonard Bernstein came out of nowhere to conduct the New York Philharmonic as a last-minute replacement for Bruno Walter, thus beginning his illustrious career. But Bernstein was five years older at the time, and had never written a *Midsummer Night's Dream* Overture.

The British simply couldn't do enough to show their admiration for young Mendelssohn. He was invited to dinners and galas and balls. The Philharmonic Society made him an honorary member. One day the governor of the British colony of Ceylon in the Pacific called upon him to propose that he compose a festival anthem for the natives, in honor of their emancipation. Felix, who kept his head through all this adulation, was vastly amused by the governor's offer, and promptly began signing his letters with the title "Composer to the Island of Ceylon." Unfortunately, he never wrote the song.

To the British, Mendelssohn was more than just a talented newcomer. He seemed to them, despite his youth, a truly great composer. Beethoven had died just two years before, and more than one British critic regarded Felix as his most likely successor.

Certainly he gave them the impression of being an innovator and a bringer of new ideas. Works like the *Midsummer Night's Dream* Overture and the Octet scherzo were fresh and original. His piano playing was not only technically remarkable, but it had a lyrical and personal touch. "His fingers *sang*," wrote one critic, while another added: "Scarcely had he touched the keyboard than something that can only be described as similar to a pleasurable electric shock passed through his hearers and held them spellbound." Much the same effect was produced when he played the organ in Saint Paul's Cathedral before a huge audience that cheered and waved to him in appreciation.

But it was as a conductor that Felix really created a sensation on his first visit to London. The art of conducting was just coming into flower. In fact, conductors in the modern sense hardly existed. Until quite recently orchestras had been led by a pianist signaling from his keyboard, or by the first violinist trying to play and beat time at once, or by a composer waving a rolled-up piece of paper. Sometimes all three operated at once, to the confusion of the players and the detriment of the music.

About ten years previously, the baton—a small, slender wand made of wood—had been introduced to England by a German composer named Ludwig Spohr. Mendelssohn also used a baton, and he insisted upon directing the orchestra himself, with no help from the first violinist or anyone else.

Felix had an elegant white baton made especially for himself in London. The English woodcarver he engaged for the job couldn't understand what the stick was for. He thought that Mendelssohn must be an alderman or other public official, and that the baton was a symbol of office. So he engraved a little crown on it. Later Felix had a baton made from white whalebone.

Felix astonished his English audiences by conducting and playing the piano without a score in front of him. His musical memory was prodigious; he knew all the Beethoven symphonies by heart. But since it seemed to bother his audiences to see him conducting without music, he decided to leave the score on the desk in front of him, and turn the pages without looking at them. Once one of the players happened to notice that the score was upside down; when he pointed it out, Felix merely smiled and went on conducting.

In many ways, Felix Mendelssohn was the first modern conductor, the prototype of a line that extends right down to Arturo Toscanini and Leonard Bernstein in our own day. It was more than a matter of baton technique or of musical knowledge; it also involved the force of his personality and his ability to motivate other people.

Felix was a handsome, well-proportioned youth, but he stood only five feet six inches tall and had a slender build. Nevertheless, he brought a commanding presence to his conducting and had a magnetic effect on his players and his audience. He knew how to get the effects he wanted with a flick of a finger or a nod of his head. One observer said that he seemed to communicate "by electric fluid" his conception of a work to an orchestra.

He also knew how to be sarcastic and cutting, even while preserving his underlying amiability and respect for his colleagues. At a rehearsal of Beethoven's Eighth Symphony with the London Philharmonic, the players simply couldn't make the Scherzo movement sound the way he thought it should. Felix tapped his baton on the stand and told the orchestra, "I know every one of you gentlemen is capable of performing, and even composing, a scherzo of your own, but right now I would like to hear Beethoven's, which I think also has some merits."

After the orchestra played it again, Felix said, "Beautiful, charming, but still too loud in two or three places. Let's take it again, from the middle."

"No, no," someone called out from the orchestra, "we'll play it all over again, for our own satisfaction."

This time they played so flawlessly that Felix laid aside his baton and just stood there listening. "If only Beethoven could have heard his music so well understood and magnificently played," he told them.

On another occasion Mendelssohn told a British women's chorus he was rehearsing, "Very good; for the first time, extremely good. But because it *is* the first time, let's try it again."

Not all the music Felix heard in England was on so elevated a plane. A group of street musicians known as the Marylebone Band made a practice of appearing outside his lodgings daily, usually just as he was sitting down to compose or to play the piano. A friend arriving one day just as the morning session started found him standing at the top of the stairs and calling out "in anguished tones" to his landlord's son, "Henry, Henry! Send them away! Here is a shilling!" Folk music of any kind never appealed to Mendelssohn. He regarded it mostly as a fake, and impartially denounced "Scotch bagpipes, Swiss cow-horns, Welsh harps."

Mendelssohn wound up his first trip to Britain by taking a pleasure jaunt through Scotland and Wales with Klingemann. The two young men had an exuberant time, wandering through the highlands, visiting Edinburgh and Glasgow, and even paying a brief call on the old poet Sir Walter Scott at his estate in Abbottsford.

It was an exhilarating trip for Felix, and it led directly to two of his most beautiful works, the *Scotch* Symphony and the *Hebrides*, or *Fingal's Cave*, Overture. The idea for the *Scotch*

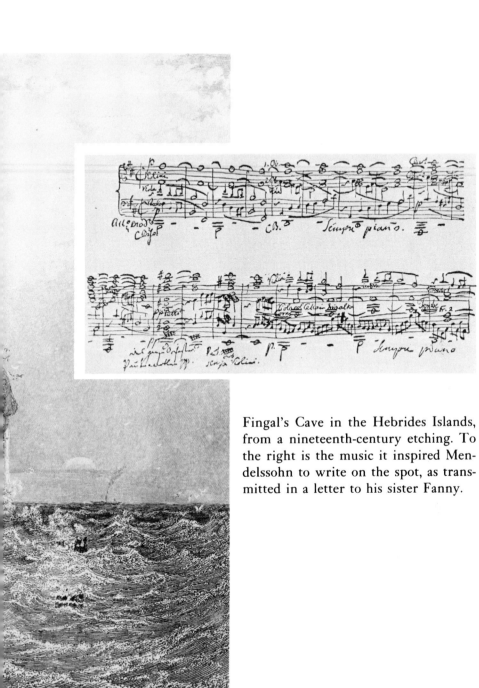

Fingal's Cave in the Hebrides Islands, from a nineteenth-century etching. To the right is the music it inspired Mendelssohn to write on the spot, as transmitted in a letter to his sister Fanny.

Symphony, a work of brooding melancholy with a triumphant conclusion, came to him while he was visiting Holyrood Castle in Edinburgh, so closely connected with the unfortunate Mary, Queen of Scots. However, far from composing the symphony on the spot, Felix worked on it on and off for twelve years before he completed it to his satisfaction and published it as his Symphony no. 3 in A Minor.

The *Hebrides* Overture was a different matter. Fingal's Cave is a basalt cavern on the tiny island of Staffa in the Hebrides. Then as now it was a famous tourist attraction reached only by ship. To get there Felix underwent another bout with his old enemy, seasickness. But he felt the journey had been worth it, for the craggy, lonely site filled him with romantic visions of surging seas, storm-tossed ships, pirate lairs, heroic sailormen, and the grandeur of nature itself. All this he depicted in his music. Although the *Hebrides* Overture takes only ten or twelve minutes to play, it remains one of the greatest seascapes in all music. Felix wrote out its surging opening theme in a letter he sent to Fanny the night he returned to shore.

On the Grand Tour

Felix's original plan had been to return home to Berlin immediately after his jaunt to Scotland with Klingemann. But the unexpected intervened in the form of a London traffic accident. A small carriage in which Felix was a passenger overturned in the street, badly injuring his knee. For two months he lay in bed while his English admirers plied him with books, flowers, fruit, and conversation. To help pass the time he grew a set of sidewhiskers.

As it turned out, the injury left no permanent effect on him. But it was annoying nonetheless, for the delay in returning meant that he would miss one of the big events in Mendelssohn family affairs—the wedding of his sister Fanny on October 3, 1829.

Fanny was marrying a painter named Wilhelm Hensel whom she had known for some six years. She might have married him far sooner had her parents not opposed the match. They were skeptical of whether Hensel could support her and were afraid he might be too much of a Bohemian. Hensel kept showering them with portraits he made of Fanny and other members of the family, until they finally were convinced of both his skill as an artist and his personal reliability.

Although Fanny, who was twenty-four, looked forward to

her marriage, she was unhappy because she knew it would draw her further away from her brother. She was particularly upset that Felix could not come to the wedding. In fact, the impish Rebecca wrote to Felix: "Last night during charming conversation by the side of the most ardent beloved, Fanny fell asleep. . . . Why? Because you are not here."

From London Felix did his best to assure Fanny that his affection for her would never diminish: "This is the last letter that will reach you before the wedding and for the last time I address you as Miss Fanny Mendelssohn Bartholdy. . . . Live and prosper, get married and be happy . . . remain yourselves, you two, whatever storms may rage outside. . . . Whether I address my sister henceforth as Mademoiselle or Madame means little."

To help celebrate his return home, and to introduce his new brother-in-law Hensel to the ways of the Mendelssohn family, Felix returned with a miniature operetta he had composed called *Son and Stranger*. It was a pleasant little work about an elderly couple whose long-lost son returns to their village in disguise. Various comic contretemps occur before he divulges his true identity so that all may end happily.

The "production" of this little work was strictly for family and friends, with Devrient singing the principal part. Felix also included a role for Hensel, but since the newest member of the family was totally unmusical, the part consisted of a single note, an F, which had to be sung over and over again for a total of ninety-one times. Poor Hensel strove his best, and everybody in the family tried to help by whistling and singing the F to him for days in advance. But when the night of the performance came, he still managed to spoil the part by missing the note most of the time. Hensel must have thought he had married into a family of musical lunatics. Nevertheless, he managed to fit in comfortably to their style of life. He and Fanny took over a small house that stood in the vast Mendelssohn garden, and he gave art lessons there. A few years later, when Rebecca married a mathematician named Gustav Dirichlet, they too took up residence in the spacious confines of 3 Leipzigerstrasse.

The trip to England had been phase one of Felix's Grand Tour, and now, after a three-month rest at home, he was ready for phase two, consisting of journeys to Italy and France.

On his way south he stopped first at Weimar to see for the last time Goethe, now in his eightieth year. The old sage once more made a fuss over Felix. He commissioned an artist to paint his portrait, quizzed him eagerly about his travels, and invited the young girls of Weimar to a dance in his honor. Above all, he made him play the piano for him. It always is difficult for us to picture a past in which the only way to hear music was to have it actually performed in one's presence. Goethe kept Felix playing hour after hour. He wanted to hear mostly Mendelssohn's music, but Mendelssohn played him mostly Beethoven's. When Felix finally left to continue his travels, he took with him as a farewell gift an autographed sheet of the manuscript of Goethe's masterpiece, *Faust*. He also promised Goethe to set to music another of the poet's works, the poem *The First Walpurgis Night*, a project which took him some years to finish.

Felix kept his eyes open and his pen busy as he traveled south. He was fascinated by the sights and sounds of the cities he passed through, and bombarded his family with letters about them. By now he had sharpened his own tastes and gained confidence in his own opinions. Some of the reports he sent home about the musical conditions he encountered were not very flattering. In Vienna, for example, he found that the music of great composers like Haydn, Mozart, and Beethoven was being ignored in favor of that of lesser men like Hummel, Field, and Kalkbrenner. Vienna, he wrote, was "a frivolous dump."

In October 1830, Mendelssohn arrived in the Italian peninsula, and he spent the next eight months there. He haunted the art galleries of Florence and Venice and made excursions to Naples and Pompeii. He settled in Rome and discovered, to his surprise, that he was well known there. "My looking-glass is stuck full of visiting cards, and I spend every evening with a fresh acquaintance," he wrote.

Felix didn't much care for the Italian music he heard. He was too much of a good German to appreciate the relatively uncomplicated melodiousness of the southerners. Besides, he complained, all the best Italian opera singers had gone north to sing in London or Paris, where there was more money to be earned.

While in Rome Mendelssohn began writing down ideas for his *Italian* Symphony, though this work, like his *Scotch* Symphony, took some time to complete. For all his aversion to the native Italian music, he managed to express in this symphony the bright sunlight and tempestuous gaiety he found in the land and its people. The *Italian* still is the most popular and frequently played of the Mendelssohn symphonies.

The most interesting musical personage Mendelssohn met in Rome was not an Italian but a Frenchman—the composer Hector Berlioz. Then twenty-seven years old, Berlioz was in Italy because he had won the Prix de Rome, France's top award to promising composers. Berlioz was the *enfant terrible* of French music, writing bold, unconventional works for vast orchestras and odd combinations of instruments. Unlike Felix, he had little regard for classical forms and musical traditions.

In fact, there was so little in common musically between these two young men that it is a little strange that they should have become such good friends. But Felix's qualities of leadership, which stood him in such good stead on the conductor's podium, carried over into his personal relations. He had his rivals and his detractors, but somehow he was always the one to whom other young musicians turned for advice, encour-

Hector Berlioz, French composer whom Felix met in Rome. They became friends and later exchanged batons.

agement, and guidance. Later on it would be Frederic Chopin and Robert Schumann; now it was Hector Berlioz. In Rome Berlioz took to lounging around Felix's workroom. Sometimes in the afternoon the two went for long walks through the Roman ruins, discussing life, art, and religion as ardently as only young men can. Recalled Berlioz afterward: "Mendelssohn believed firmly in his Lutheran religion and I sometimes shocked him profoundly by laughing at the Bible."

Felix was anxious to have Berlioz's opinion of his works. He played him *The First Walpurgis Night* and the *Hebrides* Overture at the piano. Berlioz admired both the music and Mendelssohn's playing. Like many others, he particularly admired Felix's ability to achieve orchestral effects on a keyboard. Later on, Berlioz told friends that Mendelssohn "was a little too fond of the dead"—meaning that he revered Bach and Mozart too much. But he always retained his affection and respect for him.

Felix was more than a little perplexed by his friend, for though he liked Berlioz as a person, he never really understood his tempestuous music. Berlioz himself spoke deprecatingly of one of his own pieces, *Sardanapalus*, with which he had won his Prix de Rome. He admitted to Felix that he thought its allegro section was particularly weak. "Ah, good!" said Felix, possibly overenthusiastically. "I congratulate you on your taste! I was afraid you were pleased with that allegro, and honestly, it is wretched!"

Felix spent New Year's Day of 1831 in Rome. The revelry of the holiday seemed to depress him and awaken remembrances of his Jewish ancestry. He wrote to his friend Klingemann in England that he thought holidays like New Year's Eve and New Year's Day should be celebrated solemnly rather than frivolously: "The two days are real days of atonement, and one should experience them all alone with oneself and not be afraid of grave thoughts."

In June of 1831 Mendelssohn turned northward from Rome and began his return journey. He made some interesting stopovers. In Milan he met a woman named Baroness Dorothea von Ertmann, who had once been a pupil of Beethoven, and also Karl Mozart, son of the great Wolfgang Amadeus. Karl was a minor consular official in Milan. Felix, deeply moved at meeting Mozart's son, played for him the *Don Giovanni* and *Magic Flute* overtures on the piano.

Felix lingered longer in Munich, for the simple reason that for the first time in his life he had fallen in love. The girl was a seventeen-year-old pianist named Delphine von Schauroth, whom he had met briefly while passing through the city the previous year. Now, on his return trip, he spent more and more time with her. She was beautiful, came of a substantial family, and—very important to Felix—was an excellent musician. People who watched the two of them dancing at social gatherings or strolling through the parks together thought they made an uncommonly handsome couple. They also played four-handed piano sonatas together, and once Delphine asked the young composer to hold down a high A-flat for her. "My little hand cannot reach it," she told him with an arch smile. Felix seized upon his romance with Delphine to write a characteristic bantering letter to his sister Fanny, first arousing her jealousy, then soothing it away:

> *My darling little sister:* One thing is certain: that you are a capital creature and know something of music. I felt the truth of that last night while flirting very considerably. For your brother is as foolish as you are wise, and last night he was trying to be very sweet. . . . the girl plays very well. . . . But yesterday morning, when I heard her alone, and again admired her very much, it came into my mind that we have a young lady in our garden-house whose ideas of music are somehow of a different kind, and that she knows more music than many ladies together, and I thought I would write to her and send her my best love. It is clear that you are this young lady, and I tell you, Fanny, that there are some of your pieces the mere thought of which makes me quite tender and sincere. . . . you know really and truly why God has created music, and that makes me happy.

Apparently Felix considered the possiblity of asking Delphine to marry him; he was, after all, nearly twenty-two years old and might easily have done so. He even informed his father in a letter that the king of Bavaria, who happened to be attending a ball with the young couple, had suggested "that I should marry Fräulein von Schauroth: that would be an excellent match." Felix hinted that he was annoyed by the royal suggestion, but he may really have been floating a trial balloon in the direction of the family. If so, the answer was negative, for Felix departed from Munich shortly thereafter, leaving Delphine behind. Eventually she married someone else.

However, he did memorialize his first love in his music, for while in Munich he composed one of his most popular piano works, the Concerto no. 1 in G minor, and dedicated it to Delphine von Schauroth.

Felix spent the winter of 1831-32 in Paris. When he had visited it last, at the age of sixteen, he had found it essentially frivolous and empty, and now it seemed little changed to him. Felix never really liked the French capital; London was his city. Parisian musical life was dominated by Giacomo Meyerbeer, a German-Jewish operatic composer who had undergone a transplantation to France and was prospering there. Mendelssohn disliked Meyerbeer. Perhaps he was jealous of Meyerbeer's success as an operatic composer. In any case, when somebody told him that he bore a facial resemblance to Meyerbeer, Felix promptly went out and got a short haircut so as to look different.

In Paris Felix gave a concert with the famous Conservatoire Orchestra, conducting his *Midsummer Night's Dream* Overture and appearing as piano soloist in Beethoven's Concerto no. 4 in G Major, one of his favorite pieces. But he fared less well when he tried to get the Conservatoire Orchestra to perform his *Reformation* Symphony. This work had been written some years earlier in celebration of the anniversary of the Augsburg Confession, a statement of the doctrines of the Lutheran Church. Although the *Reformation* Symphony today seems to us a perfectly straightforward and melodious piece, the members of the Conservatoire Orchestra rejected it. They said it was "much too learned" and had "too little melody." Incidents like this show the falsity of the picture often presented of Felix Mendelssohn as a composer who suffered no disappointments and whose path always was smooth.

Despite such setbacks, Felix managed to have a fine time in Paris—as most young men do. The city was filled with young musicians, many of whom were leading a gay, Bohemian existence. Some of them were destined to become famous. One was Frederic Chopin, a young pianist from Poland, just finding himself as both a performer and a composer. Another was Franz Liszt, a dashing Hungarian, at the outset of his career as the most flamboyant musical personality of the generation.

Felix's closest friend in Paris was Ferdinand Hiller, a young pianist with a background remarkably similar to his own. Like Felix, he came of a wealthy Jewish family, although

Frederic Chopin, who turned to Felix for advice and assistance when he was a struggling young pianist in Paris.

they lived in another German city, Frankfurt. He, too, had been a child prodigy; he had even been taken to Vienna to meet Beethoven, a few days before the master's death. He had been living in Paris for three years now, and he gladly took Felix under his wing, guiding him about the city much as Karl Klingemann had done in London.

It was due to Hiller that Felix met most of the town's young musicians. Hiller recalled an occasion when one of the most distinguished musical foursomes of all time gathered around a café table on the Boulevard des Italiens—Mendelssohn, Chopin, Liszt, and Hiller himself. They all were young men in their twenties, full of zest and exuberance. As they sat there over their drinks, they happened to see a rather stiff and pompous musician named Friedrich Wilhelm Kalkbrenner passing by. He was considerably older than they, and one of the most fashionable and superficial pianists of the day. The young men resolved to have some fun with him, so they beckoned him over to their table and insisted that he join them. Then they began to bombard him with "such a volley of talk" that, according to Hiller, he finally got up in despair and fled—doubtless fulminating about the disrespect of the younger generation.

Chopin told Felix that he was taking lessons from Kalkbrenner, and Felix, horrified at the idea, told the young Pole that he already played better than the pedant. Besides, he said, Kalkbrenner might well injure Chopin's highly individualistic style. Chopin followed Felix's advice, stopped going to Kalkbrenner, and gave a concert of his own music at the Salle Pleyel. Felix was in the audience and led the ovation that greeted Chopin's playing. Thus Chopin became another of the young European musicians who came to look upon Mendelssohn as their leader and spokesman.

Being so close to England, Felix couldn't resist the temptation to make a second trip to his favorite city, London, which he fondly called "that great smoky nest." Once again, its

Above, view of London in 1827 shows it as the "great smoky nest" that Mendelssohn loved.   Below, Regent's Park in London. From a sketch made by Felix during his visit in 1833.

reception was tumultuous. Soon after his arrival he walked into the hall where the Philharmonic was rehearsing. One of the players spotted him and called out, "There is Mendelssohn!" whereupon the entire orchestra began to applaud and cheer. Just as things were quieting down another musician shouted, "Welcome to him!" and the tumult started all over again. Felix had to make a little speech of thanks before the rehearsal could resume.

So happy was he in London that he remained throughout the spring, scoring one triumph after another. The *Hebrides* Overture was a particular hit with British audiences. Felix presented the Philharmonic Society with the manuscript score of it. They responded by giving him an engraved silver plate. Strangers stopped him in the street and shook his hand. Furthermore, people more and more began playing his own music at home, on their own pianos, as well as listening to it in the concert hall. He began composing a series of delightful piano pieces, called *Songs Without Words*, which were admirably suited to the keyboard yet possessed a liquid singing quality. Some of them became almost incredibly popular, like the "Spinning Song," the "Spring Song," and several "Venetian Gondola Songs." English girls, especially, loved to play them —sometimes quite badly—in their drawing rooms. While their popularity has somewhat diminished today, they still are among the favorite pieces of many a young pianist.

Felix was once asked what his *Songs Without Words* really meant, and he replied with the following cryptic "explanation":

> People often complain that music is ambiguous
> ... whereas everyone understands words. With me,
> it is exactly the reverse—not merely with regard to
> entire sentences, but also to individual words.
> These, too, seem to me so ambiguous, so vague, so
> unintelligible when compared with genuine music,

which fills the soul with a thousand things better than words. What the music I love expresses to me is not too *indefinite* to be put into words, but on the contrary, too *definite*.... If you ask me what *my* idea is, I say—just the song as it stands. . . .

As on his former visits, Felix made dozens of new friends in London. His favorites this time were the Horsley family of Kensington, whose ranks included three pretty sisters. The girls were young, vivacious, and musical, and Felix spent a good deal of time with them. But apparently he could be a very demanding person at times, because one of the Horsley girls wrote: "Mama and Mary think Mendelssohn will never marry. I do, that is, if he does not plague his mistress to death before the day arrives."

Felix might have remained in England even longer. But in the early summer Fanny wrote him an urgent letter. His old teacher Zelter had died, she reported, thus leaving open his position as head of the Singakademie, the great choral institution where Felix had presented the *St. Matthew Passion*. The board of trustees was looking for a new director, and Fanny and the rest of the family wanted Felix to apply for the post. So, very reluctantly, he said goodbye to his friends in England and returned to Berlin. The Grand Tour was over.

The First Battle of Berlin

Felix, who was now twenty-three years old, didn't come back to Berlin with any great enthusiasm. He was glad to be back with his family, of course, but after London and Paris, the Prussian capital seemed smaller and less stimulating than ever.

Nor was he certain that he wanted to be the head of the Singakademie. To be sure, the post was an important one, and as director, he would be able to present a good deal of Bach and other great music. But, as he knew all too well from his own experience with the institution, the Singakademie was run by a group of narrow-minded, ultraconservative trustees. It was only after great hestitation that he permitted his parents, his sisters, and his friend Eduard Devrient to talk him into announcing his availability for the post.

His principal opponent was a much older man named Karl Friedrich Rungenhagen, who had been Zelter's assistant for many years. Conservative, unadventurous, and "safe," Rungenhagen was the preferred candidate of the Akademie's old guard.

By way of showing interest in the position, Felix engaged the Singakademie's concert hall to give three concerts, at which he played many of his own works. Some who attended thought the music was admirable, but others regarded the concerts as an attempt by the young composer to show off.

In fact, as the date for the selection—which was to be decided by open vote of the Singakademie membership—drew near, Rungenhagen's faction mounted an increasingly vitriolic campaign against Felix. His age, his inexperience, and his long absence from Berlin were all cited against him. It was even said that his banker father was trying to "buy" the Singakademie for him. In vain his supporters argued that he was the most exciting young musician produced by Berlin in many years, that he had gained international stature in an unheard-of time, and that he could revitalize the Singakademie's traditions.

On top of everything else, Mendelssohn's Jewish birth came into the picture. Devrient reported that he heard one member say that "the Singakademie was a Christian institution and that on this account it was an unheard-of thing to try to force a Jewish lad upon them as a conductor."

Finally, in January 1833, the crucial night came, with some two hundred fifty members gathering for the final debate and vote in the Singakademie hall. The entire Mendelssohn family, including Felix, was there. Each member was called upon to announce his vote individually. At first, as the Mendelssohns listened tensely, the tally seemed fairly even. But slowly the Rungenhagen votes began to mount, and it became obvious that Felix was falling badly behind. The final tally was Rungenhagen 144, Mendelssohn 88. To top off the evening, Felix was offered the vice-directorship, which he politely declined. The next day Felix's father and the rest of the family, angered by the rebuff and the hostility shown them, resigned en masse from the Akademie.

If it was any consolation to Felix, the choice of Rungenhagen proved disastrous for the Singakademie, for under his plodding leadership it went into a steady decline, eventually losing the premier place it held among Berlin's musical institutions.

However, Felix wasted little time brooding. Fortunately, two excellent offers from the outside reached him just as Berlin was rejecting him. The city of Düsseldorf invited him to take charge, first, of a Lower Rhine Music Festival it was sponsoring, and then to remain there in charge of its year-round musical activities. And from his old friends, the Philharmonic Society of London, came an offer of 500 guineas, the equivalent of $2,000, to write a symphony, an overture, and a vocal composition for performance in England.

So hardly was the debacle of the Singakademie over then Felix was on his way to London again. The works he took with him included nothing less than his *Italian* Symphony, which he had been revising ever since his days in Rome and which he now felt was at last ready for performance. The music was acclaimed instantly by the English audiences, with one critic calling it "a composition that will endure for the ages, if we may presume to judge such a work on a single performance." Mendelssohn himself regarded it as "the most mature thing I have ever done."

Felix remained in London only a few weeks, for he now had to go to Düsseldorf to prepare for the festival. Held in May, it was one of the earliest and most colorful of all music festivals. Düsseldorf, a small city on the Rhine, was always jammed at festival time. People traveled there from a wide area, crowding the streets and shops and sleeping eight and ten in a room. The festival hall, which seated 1,300, was about a mile outside of town. People either came out on foot or arrived in carriages and farm wagons. Fire engines were sent out daily to keep the dusty roads watered down so that people could travel comfortably.

Felix knew that his father had been bitterly disappointed by the outcome of the Singakademie affair, so he invited Abraham to watch him direct at Düsseldorf. Abraham, though only in his fifties, was beginning to fail somewhat in health, with his eyesight expecially troublesome. Nevertheless, he came and was delighted by what he saw.

Felix, young as he was, took charge of proceedings with all the aplomb and sureness he had exhibited in London. The principal work to be performed was Handel's *Israel in Egypt*, which, like the *St. Matthew Passion*, had lain dormant since its composer's death.

Abraham Mendelssohn was impressed not only by the music but by the informal, democratic air of the festival itself. His words almost seem to describe the spirit of some of today's summer festivals. The audience, he reported, consisted of all types of people. At the intermissions, which were quite long, everybody rushed into a garden area, where tables and chairs had been set up, to consume "quantities of bread and butter, May wine, seltzerwater, curds and whey, etc. . . . Here they have no court, no General-Musikdirektor, no royal this-or-that. It is a true public festival."

Most of all, Abraham marveled at the organizational skills displayed by his son, whom he had never before seen operate on such a large scale. When Felix felt that the men of the orchestra were taking too long to tune their instruments he spoke to them sharply, and they speeded up. When he heard the audience chattering during one piece, he turned round and asked them to listen more quietly, and they respectfully fell silent. To Abraham, observing the alacrity with which the performers followed Felix's directions, it appeared "like a miracle that 400 persons of all sexes, classes and ages, blown together like snow before the wind, should themselves be conducted and governed like children by the youngest of them all, too young almost to be a friend to any of them, and with no title or rank whatever."

Far from resenting Felix, the performers responded to him with affection and enthusiasm. The girls of the chorus in *Israel in Egypt* decided to play a surprise on him at the opening concert of the three-day festival. All through the performance they kept roses, carnations, and other flowers hidden beneath their robes. Then at the end, as the applause surged up from the audience, they showered him with the blossoms. One girl rushed up to him carrying a laurel wreath on a velvet cushion. She placed the wreath on his head while the audience cheered. Embarrassed, Felix removed it. But no sooner did he take it off that she replaced it, until finally he gave up and took his bows wearing the crown.

The incident reminded Abraham of a legend that the Mendelssohn family possessed royal blood as descendants of one Saul Wahl, a fabled one-night king of Poland. According to this tale, a dispute between two factions of nobles in sixteenth-century Poland prevented the throne from being filled. Since there was a law that it might not remain empty even for a minute, it was agreed to install a young Jewish scholar named Saul Wahl as temporary king. According to one version, he reigned only overnight and was executed the next morning. Mendel Dessau, father of Moses Mendelssohn, was alleged to have been descended from Saul Wahl. Abraham Mendelssohn didn't believe the story, but he loved to tell it. And now he saw his own son crowned with a laurel that was likely to far outlast Saul Wahl's.

Since his father had so enjoyed the Düsseldorf experience, Felix invited him to go with him for a short vacation to England, which he had decided to visit once again. Abraham's eyesight was growing steadily worse, but Felix assured him that London was like no other city on earth, that he had wonderful friends there, and that the two of them could have a fine time attending concerts, visiting art galleries, and seeing the sights. Abraham went along, but while he reveled in the adulation which his son received, the city did not appeal to him greatly. In one letter he wrote that he had awakened on a foggy day in July and been told by his barber that it was a fine morning. " 'Is it?' I asked. 'Yes, a very fine morning,'

and so I learned what a fine summer morning is like here."
The Mendelssohns seemed accident-prone in England, for
Abraham injured his leg when he slipped during a tour of
Portsmouth Dockyard, delaying their homeward journey a
full month.

As usual, Felix himself had a swinging time in London. He
even created some gossip by his attentions to the operatic
soprano Maria Malibran. This was the same Malibran who
had so enchanted Felix on his first night in London five years
before, when he went to hear her in Rossini's *Otello*.

Now she was twenty-six and he twenty-five. She had had
a tempestuous career. Her father, the famous singer Manuel
Garcia, had married her off to an aged wealthy husband when
she was eighteen. She had run away from him, however, and
taken up with a Belgian violin virtuoso named de Beriot. She
was beautiful, talented, and strong-willed, which made her an
intriguing personality to Felix, as to almost everyone else in
the music world.

Felix was introduced to her at an evening party given by
his Kensington friends, the Horsleys. All the musical guests
were invited to perform. Malibran first sang some sacred
music, but then switched to a more popular vein, singing
Spanish, French, and English songs. Felix couldn't take his
eyes off her, and began requesting encores. Finally, she asked
him to play the piano for her. But he suddenly became self-
conscious, probably because he knew everybody was watching them, and protested that he couldn't possibly think of
following *her*. He even tried to slip into another room, but
Malibran dived right in after him and came out a moment or
two later clutching him by the arm. Felix sat down at the
piano, but instead of playing his own music, performed a
series of brilliant improvisations on the songs Malibran had
sung. The evening ended with Malibran singing more Spanish and French music to Felix's accompaniment. But although Felix saw her a few more times in London, he does

not appear to have pursued their friendship further. Three years later Malibran died from injuries suffered in a fall from a horse.

One other event of Felix's summer vacation in England merits recording. The House of Commons was debating a measure designed to remove the lingering legal restrictions on the Jews of Britain. Felix eagerly went to Parliament to sit in on the debate. In a letter home on July 23, 1833, he wrote exultantly: "This morning the Jews were emancipated. This makes me proud. . . . [The vote was] 187 ayes and 52 noes. This is noble and beautiful and fills me with gratitude to the Heavens."

This was one of the many times in his life that Felix remembered he was Moses Mendelssohn's grandson.

Once again, Felix would have been content to stay on in England. But he had accepted the permanent position in Düsseldorf to begin that autumn, and besides, his father, fully recovered from his leg injury, was anxious to get home.

For some reason, Abraham took it into his head to play a prank on the family by telling them that Felix was not returning just yet and that in his place he was bringing home with him a charming young French painter he had met named Alphonse Lovie.

It seems hard to believe that the family took the story seriously, but apparently they did. In any case, "Alphonse Lovie" of course turned out to be Felix Mendelssohn, and both father and son received a warmly affectionate homecoming.

Mendelssohn took up his full-time duties in Düsseldorf in the fall of 1833, and he remained there two years. It was not an easy time for him for he was expected to run all the town's musical activities, symphonic, operatic, and ecclesiastical.

He was disturbed at the outset when he discovered that

his advent would mean the displacement of the former director of church music, an old man who had held the post for many years. This is how Felix described this distressing event in a letter to his family:

> A very crabbed old musician in a threadbare coat was summoned. When he came and they attacked him, he declared that he neither could nor would have better music; if any improvement was required, someone else must be employed; that he knew perfectly well what vast pretensions some people made nowadays, everything was expected to sound so beautiful—this had not been the case in his day, and he played just as well now as formerly. I was really very reluctant to take the affair out of his hands, though there could be no doubt that others would do infinitely better; and I could not help thinking how I should myself feel were *I* to be summoned some fifty years hence to a town-hall, and spoken to in this strain, and a young greenhorn snubbed me, and my coat were seedy, and I had not the most remote idea why the music should be better; and I felt rather uncomfortable.

Felix also found that problems arose when he tried to produce opera. He put on a performance of Mozart's *Don Giovanni*, with himself conducting, but many people in the city were strangely unreceptive to it. Operatic management problems also seemed to keep getting in the way of his own music. "When I sat down to my composing in the morning," he wrote to his mother, "every hour was punctuated with a ringing of the bell. There were grumbling choristers to be soothed, seedy musicians to be engaged: this went on all day."

The upshot was that Felix abruptly gave up his opera-theater duties in Düsseldorf. Probably the basic difficulty was that the town was really too small for him and lacked the resources he needed to achieve really satisfying results. However, Düsseldorf did give him the final touches of experience he needed in all branches of musical production, so that he was ready when an opportunity came for him to move on to one of the major musical centers of Europe—the city of Leipzig.

The Pride of Leipzig

Leipzig, the principal city of Saxony in eastern Germany, had been watching the work of Felix Mendelssohn for several years, and began putting out feelers in his direction soon after he came to Düsseldorf. The specific post offered to him was directorship of the Leipzig Gewandhaus Orchestra, but Felix knew this would mean taking charge of virtually all musical activity in the city. When friends asked him what he intended to do in Leipzig, he replied, "Everything."

Felix came to Leipzig at just the right time for the city and himself. At twenty-six, he might have been considered young for so important a position, but he was better traveled and more widely experienced than most musicians twice his age. Leipzig, a thriving business center, had a rich musical tradition. It was the city of Johann Sebastian Bach, who lay buried in the churchyard of its Johanneskirche. Its orchestra and its choirs had been famous throughout Europe.

Yet the town had been in a period of some decline just before Mendelssohn's arrival and was only just beginning to emerge, thanks to the entry of Saxony into the German Customs Union in 1834. Commerce was the lifeblood of Leipzig. The word *Gewandhaus* itself literally means "clothing hall," for the orchestra had begun by playing in the ancient market hall of the city's linen merchants.

When Mendelssohn came to Leipzig, its narrow, twisting streets, lined by houses with high pitched roofs, and its great central market square were crowded with merchants and travelers, particularly during its great commercial fairs. Then as now it was a center for book publishing, and its university was one of the most respected and influential of the nineteenth century. Goethe had described it as "a little Paris," and one of its most distinguished resident musicians, Robert Schumann, told that Franz Liszt had spoken slightingly of the city's lack of "countesses and princesses," replied, "Let him take care! We have our own aristocracy: 150 bookshops, fifty printing plants, and thirty periodicals."

Schumann himself was typical of the young, forward-looking musicians Felix found in Leipzig. Twenty-five years old, he had come there originally to study law at the university, but turned to music instead. He married Clara Wieck, the first of the great woman pianists; together they made one of the most musical couples who ever lived.

Schumann, who had yet to win fame as a composer, was a brilliant music critic. He published a journal called the *Neue Zeitschrift für Musik* ("New Periodical for Music") which was his main weapon in his war against the musical mediocrities and reactionaries of the day. He even dreamed up a fanciful organization called the League of David, dedicated to do battle against the cultural Philistines. Schumann, who knew Mendelssohn by reputation, was overjoyed at his arrival in Leipzig. In fact, he at once inscribed him on the roster of his "League," assigning him the pseudonym "Felix Meritis."

Mendelssohn fell in eagerly with Schumann, Clara Wieck, and the other young musicians. Furthermore, he found that the civic authorities really meant to keep their promise of giving him a free hand in reenergizing the city's musical life. Unlike the aristocratic circles of Berlin,

Robert and Clara Schumann, who eagerly welcomed Mendelssohn's leadership when he became musical director in Leipzig.

the people of Leipzig took him to their hearts, so that he quickly became one of the most popular and respected personalities in the city. And in return he made it the musical capital of Europe.

Right at the start, Felix won the undying affection of the Leipzig Gewandhaus Orchestra by a simple but effective method: he got for its members a long overdue pay raise. Orchestral wages were extremely low in those days. Although Mendelssohn, as a young man of a well-to-do family, might not have been expected to be too aware of the problems of underpaid musicians, actually he sympathized deeply with them. He even refused to have anything to do with a campaign to raise funds for a Bach monument in Leipzig until the men of the orchestra were assured of better conditions. Despite what Berlioz had said, in this instance, at least, Felix was not so much "fond of the dead" as he was responsive to the needs of the living. In a letter to his friend Moscheles in England, he explained his refusal to help the drive to put up the Bach memorial:

> I declined to give anything. . . . nor would you have done so, had you known all their doings and dealings in Germany with regard to monuments. They speculate with the names of great men in order to give themselves great names; they do a great deal of trumpeting in the papers, and treat us to ever so much bad music with real trumpets. If they wish to honor Handel in Halle, Mozart in Salzburg, and Beethoven in Bonn by founding good orchestras and performing their works properly and intelligently, I am their man. But I do not care for their stones and blocks as long as their orchestras are only stumbling-blocks, nor for their conservatories in which there is nothing worth conserving. My present hobby is the improvement

Old engraving shows Johann Sebastian Bach and views of Leipzig. Below is Bach monument at St. Thomas School, erected with the help of Mendelssohn.

of our poor orchestra. After no end of letter-writ-
ing, soliciting and importuning, I have succeeded in
getting the salaries raised by 500 thalers; and before
I leave them I mean to get them double that amount.
If that is granted, I will not mind their setting up
a monument in front of the St. Thomas school; but
first, mind you, the grant!

As a result of Mendelssohn's enlightened policies and skill-
ful handling of his men, the Leipzig Gewandhaus became
within a few years the best orchestra in Europe—which
meant the best in the world. It has retained its reputation for
outstanding performance to this day. Felix won not only
higher pay but a pension system for the men. He increased
the orchestra's permanent complement to fifty, which was
large for that time. He brought in new players, including one
of the foremost violinists of the day, Ferdinand David, then
twenty-six years old, as his concertmaster and principal assistant. David later provided much of the technical advice that
helped Felix write his beautiful Violin Concerto in E Minor.
It was no wonder that the University of Leipzig gratefully
conferred an honorary doctor of philosophy degree upon
Felix less than a year after his arrival in the city.

Once the economic well-being of his men had been assured,
Mendelssohn turned his attention to the Bach memorial. No
one more revered the old Cantor of Leipzig, who had lived
and worked in the city for so many years. Felix decided that
the best way he could contribute to the campaign and pay
homage to Bach at the same time was by giving an organ
recital of his music.

The concert was held in Bach's old church, Saint Thomas',
with Felix playing such great works as the Passacaglia in C
Minor. Robert Schumann was moved to write the next day:
"How well Mendelssohn understands the treatment of Bach's
royal instrument is well known, and yesterday he laid before

us nothing but precious jewels. . . . A fine summer evening shone through the church windows; even outside, in the open air, many may have reflected on the wonderful sounds, thinking that there is nothing greater in music than the enjoyment of the twofold mastery displayed when one master expresses the other. Fame and honor to the old and the young alike!"

Mendelssohn introduced to the Gewandhaus the new method of conducting he had perfected in England. Previously the Leipzig concertmaster had played standing up, relaying signals from a conductor seated at a piano. At Felix's first Gewandhaus concert the audience was somewhat taken aback to find the concertmaster seated in his place, at the head of the violin section, with Felix standing in front of the orchestra alone, baton in hand.

Schumann reported that first concert for his paper in adulatory terms, though he had doubts about the baton: "F. Meritis stepped out. A thousand eyes flew toward him in the first moment. . . . He conducted as if he had written the overture himself [as indeed he had: it was the *Calm Sea and Prosperous Voyage*] and the orchestra played it accordingly. The baton disturbed me. . . . in the symphony, the orchestra should be like a republic . . . but it was a pleasure to see how F. Meritis anticipated with his eye every shading and how he, the blessed one, swam far in front of the common herd." In time Schumann, like the rest of Leipzig, came to accept Mendelssohn's insistence that a conductor had to run an orchestra more or less like a dictator.

So great were the crowds that came out that people began to complain that the Gewandhaus was too small. It had remarkably fine acoustics, but in seating arrangement it was a most unusual structure. The audience was seated at right angles to the stage, in two sections facing each other. If they wanted to see the performers they had to twist their necks. The seats were reserved for ladies. The men stood along the backs and sides of the hall. A lady observer from England

Hall of the Leipzig Gewandhaus. The women in the audience sat in rows facing each other, while the men stood crowded around them against the walls.

compared the arrangement of benches to that on a bus and said that the women stared at each other's dresses while the men stared at the women. Over the proscenium were engraved the Latin words *Res severa verum gaudium*—"Seriousness alone is true amusement."

Mendelssohn presented the Leipzigers with a dazzling array of programs, including much music they had never heard before. He played obscure Mozart symphonies, neglected Bach concertos, unperformed works by Beethoven. Although his own music was in constant demand he never gave it an undue place on the programs. Records kept during his years in Leipzig show that Felix Mendelssohn ranked only tenth among the most frequently played performers—far behind the great masters of the past. He eagerly played the music of the young composers of the day such as his friend Schumann, two of whose symphonies he premiered at Leipzig. One of his greatest acts of discovery—almost on a par with his revival of the *St. Matthew Passion*—was his playing, for the first time anywhere, of Franz Schubert's great Symphony in C Major, which had been left in manuscript by the composer at his death. At a series of chamber music concerts organized by Felix, his friend Ferdinand David played Bach's great Chaconne for Violin, also previously unknown to the public.

Felix got the leading performers of the day to travel to Leipzig for appearances. He also gave opportunities to local luminaries, like Robert Schumann's brilliant wife Clara. After Clara had performed his own B-minor *Capriccio*, Felix wrote admiringly that she played it "like a witch."

Mendelssohn made sure that his Paris friends Chopin, Liszt, and Hiller were invited to Leipzig. Chopin and Hiller came together, and the three had a warm and convivial reunion. Not even musical differences of opinion got in the way. Mendelssohn was then working on an oratorio called *Saint Paul*, and Chopin had just written some etudes and a new concerto. Each composer utilized totally different styles. They played samples of their work to each other. It was, Mendelssohn said ruefully, "Just as if a Cherokee and a Kaffir had met to converse." Nevertheless, Mendelssohn gladly put on a miniature festival of Chopin's music at the Gewandhaus.

Felix much preferred Chopin's lyric and poetical style of playing to Liszt's pyrotechnical showmanship. Still, when Liszt came to Leipzig Felix greeted him warmly. Liszt was regarded by almost everybody (especially himself) as the greatest pianist in the world, and he conducted himself accordingly. His clothes, if possible, were even more elegant than in his Paris days, and self-assurance fairly oozed from him. Watching him charm a throng of Leipzigers at a reception, Mendelssohn nudged Hiller, who was standing near by, and said, "There's a new phenomenon, the virtuoso of the nineteenth century." When Liszt claimed he could obtain the orchestral effects of Beethoven's nine symphonies on a modern piano, Mendelssohn commented dryly to Hiller, "I'd believe it if I could only hear the first eight bars of Mozart's G-minor Symphony, with that delicate figure in the violas, sound on the piano as they do in the orchestra."

Liszt's manager tried to take advantage of the excitement over his first visit to Leipzig by raising steeply the ticket prices to his concert. People paid, but they were resentful. Realizing that Liszt's popularity had taken a sharp dip, Felix decided to restore good relations between him and his public. He staged a special concert and reception for Liszt at the Gewandhaus, to which the public was invited without charge. Punch and pastry were served, and the musical program, in Mendelssohn's own words, consisted of "Orchestra, chorus, bishop, cake, *Calm Sea and Prosperous Voyage*, Psalm, Bach's Triple Concerto (Liszt, Hiller and me), choruses from *St. Paul*, fantasy on *Lucia di Lammermoor*, *Erlkönig*, the devil and his grandmother!" Both Liszt and the audience went away happy.

A spectacular visit to Leipzig also was made by Hector Berlioz, who had not seen Mendelssohn since their encounter in Rome a dozen years previously. Berlioz walked into the Gewandhaus one afternoon as Mendelssohn was rehearsing his *Walpurgis Night*, and the two fell into each other's arms.

As Berlioz set it down later, the conversation went like this:

> MENDELSSOHN: And is it twelve years? Twelve years since we dreamed on the plains of Rome?
>
> BERLIOZ: Yes, and in the baths of Caracalla.
>
> MENDELSSOHN: Ah! Always joking! Always ready to laugh at me!
>
> BERLIOZ: No, no; I hardly ever jest now; it was only to test your memory, and see if you had forgotten all my impieties. I jest so little, that our very first interview I am going seriously to ask you to make me a present, to which I shall attach the highest value.
>
> MENDELSSOHN: What is that?
>
> BERLIOZ: Give me your baton with which you have just conducted the rehearsal of your new work.

MENDELSSOHN: Willingly, on condition that you send me yours.

BERLIOZ: I shall be giving copper for gold, but never mind, I consent.

Thus the two composers solemnly exchanged batons. Mendelssohn must have been a little dubious about the deal, for he gave up an elegant whalebone stick covered in white leather, and received in return what Berlioz himself described as a "heavy oaken staff." Berlioz, who had been reading the *Leatherstocking Tales* of James Fenimore Cooper, enclosed the following remarkable note with his baton:

> *To the Chief Mendelssohn!*
> Great Chief! We have promised to exchange tomahawks. Mine is a rough one—yours is plain. Only squaws and pale-faces are fond of ornate weapons. Be my brother! and when the Great Spirit shall have sent us to hunt in the land of souls, may our warriors hang up our tomahawks together at the door of the council chamber.

Felix, one imagines, must have taken some time to digest *that!* But he put on two magnificent Berlioz concerts, even though he had to engage extra musicians to swell the orchestra to the proportions demanded by the French composer. Berlioz was amazed by the skill of the Leipzig musicians. He also was surprised to see Mendelssohn working painstakingly with the choristers who were learning his new and difficult music.

"It grieved me," he wrote, "to see a great master and virtuoso like Mendelssohn engaged in such a menial task, although it must be said he fulfilled it with unwearied patience, all his remarks being made with perfect sweetness and courtesy." Berlioz himself would have been all the more astonished had he known how little Mendelssohn cared personally for his music.

One other composer whom Felix introduced to Leipzig— a little reluctantly—was his sister Fanny. In many ways, Felix Mendelssohn was an enlightened man, liberal in politics, tolerant in religion, and a strong believer in the dignity of the individual. But on the question of women's rights, he shared his father's narrow and uncompromising attitude. He could admire feminine talent when he saw it, such as in Clara Schumann or Maria Malibran. But on the whole he thought women should stay away from professional activities and were best off at home, caring for their families. This applied especially to his own sisters.

So although he knew that Fanny Mendelssohn Hensel was unusually gifted both as a composer and a pianist, he did not want her to display her talents in either area in public. It is hard to forgive him for this attitude, even though he lived in an era when it was shared by many other people. Fanny might play all she wished at the Sunday family musicales, but both Felix and his father resisted the idea of her hiring a hall to give a concert. Similarly, they did not wish her to publish her songs, much as they admired them. Felix told her simply that he did not want her to become involved in the sordid commercial world. As a compensation, he did publish a few of her songs under his name, and they are still listed among the works of his opus 8 and opus 10.

Poor Fanny was very much upset by this attitude. Quite rightly she regarded herself as entitled to a little self-expression. With the support of her husband, she finally asserted her independence and gave a concert in Berlin. It was a charity benefit, and she played Felix's Piano Concerto in G Minor. She herself described it whimsically as "one of those amateur affairs where the tickets are twice the usual price, and the chorus is composed of countesses, ambassadresses, and officers."

She also published two books of her songs under her own name. At this point Felix finally broke down and decided to present a song by Fanny at a concert in Leipzig. He himself played the piano accompaniment. Afterwards he wrote to her:

> How beautiful it was! You know what my opinion of it has always been, but I was curious to see whether my old favorite, which I had hitherto only heard sung by Rebecca to your accompaniment in the gray room with the engravings, would have the same effect here in the crowded hall, with the glare of the lamps and after listening to noisy orchestral music. I felt so strange when I began your soft, pretty accompaniment imitating the waves, with all the people listening in perfect silence; but never did the song please me better. The people understood it, too, for there was a hum of approbation each time the refrain returned . . . and much applause when it was over. . . . I thank you in the name of the public of Leipzig and elsewhere for publishing it against my wish.

When several other songs by Fanny were published later, Felix wrote her: "May you have much happiness in giving pleasure to others; may you taste only the sweets and never the bitterness of authorship; may the public pelt you with roses and never with stones; and may the printer's ink never draw black lines upon your soul—all of which I devoutly believe will be the case, so what is the use of my wishing it!"

A few of Fanny's other compositions, including her Trio for Piano and Strings, were printed during her lifetime. But most of her music still lies in manuscript form, unpublished and unperformed. She continues to be known to history only as the sister of Felix Mendelssohn. Perhaps she would have wished for no more.

Felix Finds a Wife

In October 1835 Felix decided to pay a visit to his family in Berlin, accompanied by his friend Moscheles, who had been staying with him in Leipzig. Since both Fanny and Rebecca were there with their husbands, a grand reunion was held at 3 Leipzigerstrasse. Abraham Mendelssohn by now was almost completely blind, but he loved the sounds of a houseful of family and friends. Felix and Moscheles regaled him with a series of piano duets that were so brilliant he could hardly tell when one left off and the other began. Everybody had a marvelous time. Finally, Felix had to return to Leipzig. He promised to come back for Christmas. When his father remarked, quite solemnly, that he hoped he would still be alive at Christmas, nobody took him very seriously.

A few weeks later, however, Abraham Mendelssohn caught a slight cold and, without warning, died in his sleep one night. Hensel journeyed alone to Leipzig to carry the sad news. Felix was grief-stricken, and rushed back with Hensel to Berlin. There he resolved to build his father a monument in music. For some time he had been planning a large-scale choral work about Saint Paul, the Apostle who spread Christianity through Europe. He now decided that he would complete *St. Paul* as a memorial to his father. The massive oratorio, written in the style of Johann Sebastian Bach, was presented for the first time at another Lower Rhine Festival in Düsseldorf in May 1836. It was widely admired in its own time, but is seldom performed complete nowadays.

Most of the Mendelssohn family traveled to Düsseldorf to attend the premiere of *St. Paul*. Fanny even sang in the chorus. It was just as well that she was there, for one of the soloists, appropriately singing the role of a False Witness, missed his cue at one point. Fanny, with her usual quick musical instincts, hissed out the right word to him and got things going again.

Fanny seized the opportunity of her reunion with Felix to have a heart-to-heart talk to him. In music she was always content to let him be the leader, but now, as an older sister and a married woman, she felt she could talk to him frankly about his personal affairs. She reminded him that he was now twenty-seven years old and the only one of Abraham's children who was still unmarried. Even his younger brother Paul had wed a cousin of the poet Heinrich Heine not long before. She recalled that their father had once said with a sigh that Felix was so finicky that he seemed unlikely to ever find either a subject for an opera, or a wife. Fanny urged him, as she prepared to return to Berlin, to think seriously about the matter.

Actually, Felix was more than ready. While he enjoyed his bachelor life in Leipzig and the mobility it gave him, he also yearned for home comforts such as he had enjoyed in his Berlin days. And he envied his sisters and his brother the warmth of their family circles.

A short time after separating from Fanny and returning to Leipzig, Felix was asked to go to the city of Frankfurt for six weeks for an emergency assignment. The conductor of the principal choral group there, the St. Cecilia Society, had fallen ill, and being a friend of Felix, requested him to take over. It turned out to be a lucky trip for Felix Mendelssohn. In the first place, his old friend Ferdinand Hiller lived in

Frankfurt, which meant he could spend a lot of time with him. In the second, the famous Gioacchino Rossini, composer of *The Barber of Seville*, was on a visit to Frankfurt, and he and Felix had a cordial encounter in which they expressed mutual admiration. Most important of all, it was in Frankfurt that he met Cecile Jeanrenaud, the girl he was to marry.

Cecile was a blonde, blue-eyed girl of French Huguenot extraction. She was eighteen years old, a talented painter, and an amateur singer. In fact, she sang in the choir of the St. Cecilia Society, where he saw her first while rehearsing a cantata by Bach and Handel's oratorio *Samson*.

Felix's actual introduction to Cecile Jeanrenaud came about in a curious fashion. Among the residents of Frankfurt at that time happened to be none other than old Dorothea Mendelssohn, Moses Mendelssohn's free-wheeling daughter and Felix's aunt. Dorothea was a widow, her husband Frederick von Schlegel having long since died. She had lived in several cities before finally settling in Frankfurt. Now in her seventies, she eagerly welcomed her famous nephew to Frankfurt. Felix, for his part, was delighted to renew his acquaintance with the old girl, for so long the pariah of his family. It so happened she was a good friend of the Jeanrenaud family, so what could be more natural than for her to introduce Felix to the pretty young girl who was singing in his choir?

Felix fell in love with Cecile almost as soon as he met her. He talked about her to Hiller for hours. He began to drop hints in his letters to his mother and sisters that he had met a girl whose "presence has given me happy days in Frankfurt at a time when I badly needed them." To settle any doubts in his own mind, he went off for a month to the seashore so that he could think things over. When he came back he was resolved to marry Cecile, and so informed his family.

For her part Cecile was a little overawed at first by her famous suitor. She had pictured Mendelssohn to be much

Felix's wife Cecile. She was eighteen at her marriage, and said to be one of the most beautiful girls in Frankfurt.

older than herself, wearing a satin skullcap and playing dreary, academic music.

The reality was much more attractive—a slender, elegant, if somewhat smallish young man with dark curly hair, deep brown eyes, and sideburns that ran down past the angle of the jaw.

Felix and Cecile went for strolls and carriage rides through the old town on the river Main. He played the piano for her and made sketches of her home and the scenery around her. Finally he took her on an excursion to Kronenthal, a nearby town noted for its picturesque setting, and there, beneath a cluster of beech trees, he asked her to marry him.

The wedding was held on March 28, 1837, in the French Reformed Church of Frankfurt. Hiller was there, and, as a surprise, composed a wedding chorus. Old Dorothea was also on hand. Felix's mother and sisters did not travel from Berlin for the ceremony, but they soon began a lively correspondence with his new wife. When they finally met Cecile, they agreed she was one of the most beautiful girls they had ever seen.

Felix Mendelssohn undoubtedly was one of the most home-loving of all composers. He quickly made his wife part of the Mendelssohn family circle. A year after their marriage, he and Cecile left Leipzig to spend the summer at the family home in Berlin. With them they brought their infant son, Carl Wolfgang Paul, the first of the five children they were to have. They moved into quarters at 3 Leipzigerstrasse. As Fanny and her family, together with Rebecca and hers, were already living there, it made for a crowded and cheerful family group.

Cecile learned some unexpected things about her husband that summer—for example, that he had a particular taste for Jewish food delicacies like *kuchen*, a kind of butter cake. "Moses must have been a great lawgiver," he told her contentedly while stuffing himself with it. Later on Cecile asked him, "But can *kuchen* be baked only by Jews?"

Mendelssohn's children were named Carl, Marie, Paul, Felix, and Lili. They were born between 1838 and 1845, and all but little Felix lived to adulthood—indeed most became quite distinguished in their fields.

Mendelssohn continued to work hard at his composing and his other musical activities after his marriage. He split his time between Leipzig and London, where he was constantly in demand. He was in close communication and contact with musicians everywhere, for by now he was the most sought-after conductor in Europe. But wherever he went, he always resented being separated from his family. The sketches and drawings he loved to make—for he was an accomplished artist —now were of his wife and children at home or on a holiday.

Felix used to rise early in the morning, usually around six. In those days of poor artificial illumination daylight was important, and he wanted to make use of it. Several people who had breakfast with him over the years recorded that he liked to dip his rolls into his coffee; apparently this was an eating habit he never lost. He seldom practiced the piano, and he liked to do his composing shut away from everybody else in his study. He always had a tremendous amount of work hanging over him, including his administrative duties and his correspondence with other musicians, publishers, and impresarios, in addition to his own composing. His friend Hiller wrote that he had "a marvelous spiritual equilibrium," otherwise he could not have worked amid so many distractions.

Mendelssohn himself took great satisfaction in his friends. Once he noted: "When from time to time I feel dissatisfied with myself, I think of this one or that who is friendly with me and I tell myself: 'You can't be so bad if such people love you.'"

Felix seems to have been a patient father who got on extremely well with his small children. Once, annoyed by something Carl had done, he gave him a slap. He was stricken with remorse and was surprised and relieved to find that Carl had forgotten all about it by the following day. He occasionally gave the children piano lessons himself. Once he got mixed up and was teaching Marie to turn the wrong finger under while playing a scale. Cecile had to come in and correct him.

He used to write to his mother and sisters proudly of the doings of the children, and his letters reflect the general family horseplay and good spirits: "Here come Cecile and Carl, the latter with a large crayfish, which he sets crawling on the floor, while Marie and Paul scream with delight. . . . even the baby looks about quite intelligently with his blue eyes." To Rebecca he wrote: "We are leading a very quiet life, for my horror of aristocratic acquaintances has if possible increased. . . . we stay home in our family circle, and that is much the best."

While it was now Felix who perferred to remain home-bound, his sisters at last had their chance to travel. Fanny went first. She and Hensel had one son, Sebastian, and the three of them set out for a leisurely tour of Italy, stopping first to visit Felix and Cecile in Leipzig.

Rebecca and her family went next, traveling with her husband Dirichlet and their two sons. She became ill while in Naples and, although she recovered, spent a long period of convalescence there, so that her Italian journey lasted over a year.

To Felix, comfortably settled in Leipzig, it was like reliving his own Grand Tour to read his sisters' letters from abroad. He kept writing them about what to see and whom to visit. He enumerated the art museums and classical monuments he had toured and made various recommendations.

But he himself felt that his own sightseeing days were over. When his children were older, he thought it might be fun to take them on similar excursions to Italy or to England. But for the moment he was well content to remain at home in Leipzig or to visit his mother in Berlin and his in-laws in Frankfurt.

He and Cecile had discovered a pleasant village named

Soden near Frankfurt. It was a spa, with mineral springs that were said to be good for dyspepsia, anemia, scrofula, and phthisis. Mendelssohn suffered from none of these ailments, but he liked the rural and quiet charm of the village, where the children could roam freely while he and Cecile painted or sketched.

In a letter he wrote to Rebecca, Felix cheerfully acknowledged that Soden might not be Palermo or Sorrento—but that he liked it just the same. It was wrong to enjoy only one kind of beauty to the exclusion of all others, he explained: "I never can bear to hear people say they appreciate Beethoven only or Palestrina only, or again, Mozart or Bach only. Give me all four, or none at all. . . . this life at Soden, with its eating and sleeping, without dress-coat, without visiting cards, without carriage and horses, but with donkeys, with wildflowers, with music paper and sketch-book, with Cecile and the children, is doubly refreshing." On another occasion, when he had been feeling worn-out and weary, he wrote after a two weeks' vacation in Soden: "If I could only go on living for half a year as I have lived the last fortnight, what might I not be able to face?"

Unfortunately for Mendelssohn, the world would not let him long enjoy such respites.

The Second Battle of Berlin

Mendelssohn's tremendous success in Leipzig, which he turned into one of the most talked about musical centers in Europe, had the effect of arousing second thoughts in Berlin. Although the Prussian capital had in effect rejected him some five years earlier, there were some who now thought he should be summoned back.

Among those who held this opinion was the new king of Prussia, Frederick William IV. He had grave faults as a ruler, but he tried his best to be known as a monarch who cultivated the arts. It disturbed him that the most famous of all German musicians, Felix Mendelssohn, should have chosen to live and work in Leipzig rather than in his capital city.

Frederick William IV even conferred upon Mendelssohn one of his highest distinctions, the order "Pour le Mérite." Felix was not terribly impressed. Shortly after the medal of the order arrived, he took a stroll with some friends across a bridge in the town of Offenbach near Frankfurt. One of the party stayed behind to pay the toll. Said the tolltaker, "Isn't that the Mr. Mendelssohn whose music we sing at our society?" Upon being told that it was indeed, the tolltaker said, "Then, if you please, I would like to pay his toll myself." Upon being informed of what had happened, Mendelssohn smiled and said, "I like that better than the Order Pour le Mérite."

The king wanted Mendelssohn to return to Berlin and run the city's musical affairs much as he was doing in Leipzig. He spoke about it to Felix's brother Paul, who, he knew, ran the family's business affairs, and asked him to serve as intermediary. Paul urged Felix to accept, as did Fanny, Rebecca, and his mother. All of them wanted him closer to home. Felix was very reluctant. He was happy in Leipzig and he had bad memories of his previous Berlin experiences. He distrusted the king and the aristocrats around him. But he was susceptible to the appeals of patriotism and also to the desires of his mother, now a widow and growing old. A long series of negotiations with the king's emissaries took place. Many promises were made to Felix, one of them being that he would be able to found a great conservatory of music in Berlin at which all kinds of students, including poor ones, would be welcome. In the end he accepted and agreed to move back. However, he didn't cut himself off completely from Leipzig. He loved the city too much to leave it altogether, and besides he wanted a lifeline to fall back upon in case things went wrong. So he retained his connection with the Gewandhaus, promising to conduct a certain number of concerts there each year.

In 1841 Felix and his family moved to Berlin. At first it was exciting and stimulating to be back. Fanny was still holding the Sunday musicales at 3 Leipzigerstrasse, and with Felix in town they became more brilliant than ever. On one occasion the audience included Franz Liszt and no fewer than eight royal princesses!

Felix also met a number of young musicians, among them Richard Wagner, then just at the outset of his career as an operatic composer. Wagner was notorious for his anti-Semitism, and in later years he was to mount a cruel attack on Mendelssohn as a Jew. Right now, however, Mendelssohn was at the peak of his power and influence, so Wagner characteristically sought him out and paid court to him. There is even a letter from Wagner which reads: "My dear, dear Mendelssohn: I am really happy that you like me. If I have come a little closer to you, it is the nicest thing about my Berlin expedition." Mendelssohn played some of Wagner's music in Leipzig and came backstage to congratulate him after a performance of his new opera *The Flying Dutchman.*

Despite the busy musical activity of Berlin, Mendelssohn was unhappy there. In fact, he spent five miserable years in King Frederick William's service, though he sometimes managed to escape for a short stay in Leipzig or a quick trip to England. Despite all the king's promises, he was seldom given the musical resources he had been promised. Many of the musicians in the royal orchestra were hostile or openly rude to him. Even worse, they were far inferior as instrumentalists to their Leipzig counterparts.

To add to the gloom of his years in Berlin, in December 1842 Leah Mendelssohn died. The passing of his mother affected Felix as deeply as that of his father. He happened to be in Leipzig when the news came, and he shut himself in his room and wept. Shortly afterward he wrote his brother Paul that he was trying to carry on his regular conducting and other duties. He said he had found some "half-mechanical work" to do, such as transcribing and copying, and that this helped him find relief from sorrow. He was grateful, he said, for "the pleasant intercourse with the old familiar oboes and violas and the rest, who live so much longer than we do, and are such familiar friends."

Considering his unhappiness there, it is no surprise that several of the works Mendelssohn wrote in Berlin to please the king turned out to be inferior to his usual product. But he also managed to compose a number of fine pieces, such as his *Variations sérieuses* for piano.

Most remarkable of all, it was in Berlin that he produced one of his greatest achievements, the completion of his *Midsummer Night's Dream* music. He had written the Overture when he was seventeen. Now, at the age of thirty-four, he was asked by the king to write a full set of incidental music for an actual production of the play.

Almost as if the seventeen intervening years had never existed, Felix sat down and wrote interludes, entr'actes, dances, a nocturne, and a wedding march to go along with the Overture. So perfect were they that they all seemed to have been written at the same time, and breathe the same spirit of eternal youth and freshness.

Even in Berlin, the *Midsummer Night's Dream* music was an instant and overwhelming success. The whole family was in attendance, scattered through the theater, for adjacent seats were hard to find. There were two rows of "Mendelssohn and Company" in the balcony, Fanny reported; and Paul said that when the audience began calling for "Mendelssohn" at the conclusion, he stood up and took a few bows himself. Shortly afterward the score was performed in Leipzig, London, and elsewhere in Europe, creating for itself in the world's musical consciousness a place that it has never lost.

Perhaps it was Fanny Mendelssohn who once again best put into words what Felix had accomplished:

> We were mentioning yesterday what an important part the *Midsummer Night's Dream* has always played in our house, and how we had all at different ages gone through the whole of the parts from Peaseblossom to Hermia and Helena, and now it has come to such a glorious ending. We really were brought up on the *Midsummer Night's Dream*, and Felix especially had made it his own, almost recreating the characters which had sprung from Shakespeare's inexhaustible genius. From the Wedding March, so full of pomp but so thoroughly festive in its character, to the plaintive music of Thisbe's death, the fairy songs, the dances, the interludes, the characters, including such creatures as clowns—all and

everything has found its counterpart in music, and his work is on a par with Shakespeare's.

Not even the success of the *Midsummer Night's Dream* could reconcile Mendelssohn to Berlin. Even when some of the aristocrats there sought to praise him they succeeded only in offending him. One of Frederick William's courtiers remarked to him at a supper at the palace after attending a *Midsummer Night's Dream* performance, "What a pity that you wasted your beautiful music on such a stupid play!" Felix was quite indignant.

In 1844 Mendelssohn finally went to the king and told him he wished to return to Leipzig. Frederick William professed to be surprised at Felix's unhappiness but finally consented, on condition that he be available for special occasions in the future. Felix agreed, and quickly moved his family back to Leipzig. "The first step out of Berlin," he told his friend Devrient, "is the first step toward happiness."

Mendelssohn was welcomed back enthusiastically when he resumed residence in Leipzig. He was able to follow through there on a project he had never been allowed to accomplish in Berlin—the establishment of a great conservatory of music. With the cooperation of the king of Saxony and local officials, the Leipzig Conservatory now came into being; it has remained one of Europe's foremost institutions of musical education.

Mendelssohn himself taught piano and composition classes in addition to administering the school. He dealt only with advanced pupils, and he could be rough on them when he thought the circumstances demanded it. "That's how cats play," he once burst out at a careless pianist. "A very ungentlemanly modulation!" he once reproved a composition student. But he wasn't above admitting his own mistakes. A favorite exercise of his was to put on the blackboard a theme and have each student write a counterpoint for it, with the task growing increasingly complicated as the exercise grew longer. On one occasion, a pupil found it impossible to add even a single note. "You can't tell where to put the next note?" asked Mendelssohn. "No," said the boy. "Well," replied Mendelssohn with a sigh, "I'm glad of that, because neither can I."

Mendelssohn gathered a distinguished faculty for his Conservatory. His concertmaster, Ferdinand David, taught violin. He induced his friend Moscheles to come from England with his wife Charlotte to take charge of the piano department. A prominent Danish composer named Niels Gade taught composition, as did Robert Schumann.

Most of all, Felix made sure that lack of money would be no impediment to worthy students seeking admission. In a memorandum to the Conservatory's financial backers he noted that "the most admirable talent" was often to be found among students who "rarely possess the means of paying for private lessons." Therefore he insisted that scholarships be available to such young musicians. Among those who responded to this opportunity was a twelve-year-old violin prodigy from Vienna named Joseph Joachim. He traveled to Leipzig, attracted by the renown and liberality of the new school. Mendelssohn immediately recognized him as possessing extraordinary talent and took him under his wing, even accompanying him at public concerts. Joachim, who lived until 1907, eventually developed into the foremost violin master of his generation.

Soon after his departure from Berlin, Mendelssohn wrote his own Violin Concerto in E Minor, one of his supreme masterpieces. He had been thinking of it, on and off, for five years, telling his concertmaster, Ferdinand David: "I should like to write a violin concerto for you. . . . One in E minor runs through my head, the beginning of which gives me no peace." David gave the Mendelssohn Concerto its world premiere and, as with the *Midsummer Night's Dream*, it was immediately hailed as a work of genius. It probably is the most popular and frequently played violin concerto in the world today.

As before, Mendelssohn continued to present to his Leipzig audiences Europe's foremost performers. One of these was a young singer he had met in Berlin. Her name was Jenny Lind and she later became world famous as "The Swedish Nightingale."

When Felix met Jenny he was thirty-five and at the pinnacle of his career, and she twenty-three and just at the beginning of hers. He heard her sing in Berlin and was tremendously impressed, for some reason singling out her F-sharp as particularly remarkable.

Jenny, for her part, was overwhelmed by Felix. Some people even thought she was in love with him. He spent hours working with her at the piano. "He is quite an exceptional man," she wrote to a friend. Felix was resolved to do all he could to help her career.

Naturally, he invited her to Leipzig to give a concert with him and the Gewandhaus Orchestra. Everybody was enchanted with her. The only problem arose when ticket prices were raised for the occasion, and the students at the Conservatory, who usually were admitted free to the concerts, couldn't get in at all. This led to a student demonstration, at which a redheaded young pianist named Otto Goldschmidt acted as spokesman. He was permitted to see the Gewandhaus' board of directors, but they declined to change their policy. So young Goldschmidt, determined to hear Jenny Lind, scraped up the money and bought a ticket. It was a momentous event for both of them, for years later he wound up as Jenny's accompanist on a trip she made to the United States under the auspices of P. T. Barnum, and in 1852 they were married.

So popular had Jenny been at her first appearance in Leipzig that another was immediately scheduled. It was a benefit for the orchestra's Pension Fund, at which Jenny sang with

Felix accompanying her. One of the numbers was his own "Spring Song."

That night, a throng of students—many of of whom had managed to get into the second concert—crowded into the courtyard of the house in which she was staying to serenade her by torchlight. They had brought their instruments with them, and they alternately played and sang to her. She listened at the window, but was apprehensive about how to respond. Then a delegation from the orchestra, led by Ferdinand David, marched upstairs to present her with a silver tray inscribed from "the grateful musicians" of Leipzig. By now poor Jenny seemed almost terrified and couldn't find words to reply.

Felix, who had been standing quietly by, came to her rescue. He took her gently by the arm, led her downstairs to the courtyard, and, turning to the students who crowded around in a circle, said, "Gentlemen, you think that this is the Kapellmeister Mendelssohn who is speaking to you, but you are wrong. It is Fräulein Jenny Lind who is speaking to you, and she thanks you from the heart for the exquisite surprise you have given her. And now I turn myself back into the Leipzig Music Director again and ask you to wish long life to Fräulein Jenny Lind. Long life to her! And again, long life to her! And, for the third time, long life!" And so, with the cheers ringing in her ears, and her reputation considerably enhanced, Jenny returned to Berlin.

The paths of Jenny and Felix crossed many times in the years ahead. He brought her back to Leipzig for another appearance the following season, and he all but took over management of her career by mail, advising her about concerts, contracts, and operatic engagements. In May 1847 they appeared together at the Lower Rhine Music Festival, held that year at Aix-la-Chapelle. Here he told her that he was writing an oratorio about the Old Testament prophet Elijah and that he wished her to take the leading soprano role. He also talked to her, almost on the same level of intimacy as to his wife and his sisters, about his own personal problems— how he felt overworked, hoped to get away from the daily routine of organizing and directing concerts, and wanted to devote more time to his compositions and his family.

He summed it all up in a letter he wrote to Jenny not long before his death: "I often think now of your question on the Rhine steamboat, whether I should not like to leave Leipzig again? And your wish that I should not stay in Leipzig forever, etcetera, etcetera. You were quite right, and I well know what you meant; and in two or three years, at the utmost, I think I shall have done my duty here, after which I should scarcely stay any longer. Perhaps I might prefer Berlin; perhaps the Rhine; somewhere where it is very pretty, and where I could compose all day long, as much as I liked. But really you would have to sing to me sometimes."

England — and America?

For a conductor nowadays to travel continually from country to country is nothing unusual. But in Felix Mendelssohn's time it was a decided novelty. Without benefit of such modern amenities as jet planes or speedy steamships he managed to shuttle between Germany and England so frequently that he exercised continual leadership in the cultural life of both lands.

Mendelssohn left an even deeper stamp upon English music than he did on German. Everywhere in England there sprang up Mendelssohn Clubs, Choirs, Societies, and Halls. Much the same thing happened in the United States, for his music was extremely popular there, too.

In England, Felix could do no wrong. Everybody from humble choristers in amateur choirs to Queen Victoria herself regarded him as the supreme composer of the day and sang his music with enthusiasm.

Mendelssohn has come to be regarded as the ideal Victorian composer, but actually he had established his popularity in England and made four trips there before the queen ever came to the throne. Victoria was crowned in 1837 at the age of eighteen. Felix was twenty-eight at the time. The Queen was something of a musical amateur herself, and her husband, Prince Albert, had even greater talents. He played the organ and composed songs, some of which are quite charming. Naturally Albert, of Germanic origin himself, was deeply interested in the music of the famous "Dr. Mendelssohn," as Felix was usually called in official British circles. So was the Queen.

To the Victorians, Mendelssohn was more than just a fine musician. He also was a glamorous foreigner who spoke their language perfectly and a model of gentlemanliness and good breeding. Even his Jewish ancestry, which had always been held against him in Berlin, was something of an asset. Full emancipation for English Jews, as we have seen, was being enacted in Parliament. Soon there would be a prime minister, Benjamin Disraeli, whose father had been a Jew and undergone conversion. The Rothschild family, with whom Felix was well acquainted, was a power in English finance. Although some English biographers harped on Mendelssohn's Lutheranism and said that he embodied Christian virtues, he was also well known for having been descended from the great Jewish philosopher Moses Mendelssohn.

Many Victorians admired Felix for his industriousness and his ability to get things done. He was more than just a dreamer, he was a doer—which was something that appealed to the practical English. If you wanted someone to organize a music festival, attract great crowds to it, and make sure everything came out successfully, Mendelssohn was your man.

For his part, Felix found England a more exciting and progressive country with each visit. He was especially enthralled by its railways, a technological development in which it was far ahead of the Continent. On a visit to Liverpool he persuaded a railway inspector to take him through a new tunnel that had just been completed on the line to Manchester. He wrote home about the mines and mills he had seen with as much enthusiasm as his visits to art galleries and museums. If it weren't for his love of Leipzig, his ties to his

My dear Madam

I shall be most happy to accept your kind invitation for Tuesday the 14th & to partake of that fine dish of Politics of which you have given me hopes. Although I think I shall leave London on Tuesday night, I hope yet to be able to avail myself of your kindness. I was extremely sorry to hear Mr. Taylor has been so seriously unwell, and hope to find him better very soon. With my best regards to him believe me — Dear Madam —

                    very truly yours

100 Gt Portland St.
7th May.
                    Felix Mendelssohn

Mendelssohn displays his command of English in a letter to a London hostess accepting her invitation to partake of a "fine dish of politics."

family, and the feeling he always had of being a good German, he might easily have settled in England for good. As it was, he put up with the necessity of commuting there regularly despite the difficult travel conditions.

In 1842 Felix's eminence in England reached its peak: he was invited to visit Queen Victoria and Prince Albert at Buckingham Palace. The queen wasn't then the matronly figure made famous in dozens of portraits. She was a slender young woman of twenty-three. Albert was the same age.

Despite their royal station, Victoria and her husband were apparently a bit nervous about meeting the famous "Dr. Mendelssohn." Albert wanted to show him a new organ that had been installed in the palace, and he knew that Felix's organ playing had created a sensation in London. As for the queen, she was determined to sing one or two of Felix's songs for him, and she didn't know how he would respond to her interpretations.

Contemporary artist depicted Mendelssohn playing at Buckingham Palace for a slim Queen Victoria and an elegant Prince Albert.

Albert was alone in the music room when Felix entered, and for several minutes the two men had an animated conversation about the new organ. Then the queen entered and as she did so a draft from the opened door blew music sheets all over the room. In a moment all three of them were on the floor picking up papers. "What a confusion!" Victoria exclaimed.

While the queen listened, Albert and Felix took turns trying out the organ. Felix played a chorus, "How lovely are the messengers," from his *St. Paul*, and Victoria and Albert promptly began singing it.

When Mendelssohn expressed his pleasure, Albert told him that Victoria also sang some of his songs, and after some urging she agreed to perform one of them right then and there. However, it developed that the queen's music had all been packed up for a journey to the country planned for later that day.

After a time, the party adjourned to the queen's sitting room, and there a bound volume of Mendelssohn's first set of songs, opus 8, was discovered.

The queen prepared to sing one, but then noticed that a large parrot was uneasily stirring about in a cage in the room.

"He had better be removed," she said, "or else he will sing louder than I do."

Albert rang the bell for a servant, but Felix himself picked up the cage and deposited it outside the door.

Then, with Felix accompanying her, Victoria began the song. She sang it charmingly, in strict time and tune, Felix reported afterwards, "except that in the phrase where it goes down to D and comes up again by semitones, she sang D-sharp each time. And as I gave her the note the first two times, the last time she sang D where it should have been D-sharp!"

As luck would have it, the song the queen had selected, "Italy," was not by Felix at all, but by Fanny Mendelssohn —one of the numbers by his sister that he had incorporated into his published works rather than letting her publish them under her own name. The queen and her consort looked considerably surprised when he told them.

"Now I beg you to sing one of *mine*," said Felix, and Victoria obliged with another song from opus 8. To conclude his visit to the palace, Felix improvised at the organ. As a memento, Albert presented him with a ring engraved "V.R. 1842." Felix gave Victoria a more durable gift in return: he dedicated his *Scotch* Symphony to her.

In a letter to his mother Felix reported the entire incident with satisfaction and good humor. He quoted a current quip that Buckingham Palace was "the one really pleasant, comfortable English house." Then he added jokingly that if anyone thought that after his visit to the palace he had become an admirer of royalty, "tell him that I vow and declare that I am a greater radical than ever."

Victoria's approval put the final seal on Mendelssohn's popularity in England—if anything further were needed. In Britain he was invigorated by a sense of well-being that he felt nowhere else. He met the novelists Charles Dickens and William Thackeray, who each pronounced him their favorite composer. He dined with bishops and noblemen. He enjoyed and reciprocated the esteem of the ordinary British concertgoer and man in the street.

"A mad, most extraordinarily mad time," he wrote to Fanny in 1844, on his eighth visit to London. "I never had so hectic a time before—never in bed till half-past one; for three days together not a single hour to myself in any one day. . . . My visit was glorious. I was never received anywhere with such universal kindness, and have made more music in these two months than I do elsewhere in two years."

Only on one occasion did the British musicians fail him—when the men of the Philharmonic refused to play Schubert's great C Major Symphony. He had premiered this long-buried masterpiece to great acclaim in Leipzig five years before. But when the British musicians tried it out at a rehearsal, they laughed out loud at its harmonies and figurations, and insisted they could not play it.

Much the same thing happened when Mendelssohn wanted them to perform a new Symphony in C Minor by Niels Gade, the Danish composer who often conducted at the Gewandhaus. Mendelssohn was so angered at the attitude of the London musicians that he refused to let them play his own *Ruy Blas* Overture, which he had brought with him to England. Mendelssohn professed never to care much for the *Ruy Blas* Overture anyhow. He regarded the Victor Hugo play for which it was written as "perfectly horrible." Since the overture itself had been composed to aid the pension fund of the Leipzig theater, he referred to it derisively as the "Overture to the *Pension Fund.*" Succeeding generations have found it a dramatic and romantic work that catches perfectly the spirit of the play.

In 1845 Mendelssohn received an invitation to come to America. This is how he described it in a letter to his brother Paul:

> I recently received an invitation to a music festival, which flattered me so much that I even *look* flattered (as Cecile tells me). It is to New York. They write in the friendliest way; claim that the return trip would take but four weeks; want to pay my entire fare plus 1,000 pounds; and arrange a concert that would bring me the same amount. They assure me that my coming would improve the whole state of music there. What a pity that for me it is as impossible as a journey to the moon!

The invitation to the United States came from the Philharmonic Society of New York, the same organization known today as the New York Philharmonic. It had been founded in 1842 by a conductor bearing the mellifluous name of Ureli

Corelli Hill. He was a violinist, born in Connecticut, who had gone to Europe to study with Ludwig Spohr and had then returned to his native land. Hill was an able musician, and he knew Mendelssohn's work very well. In 1838, conducting the New York Sacred Music Society, he gave the first performance in the United States of *St. Paul.* When he founded his Philharmonic Society, he also scheduled several of Felix's works. The third program ever given by the new orchestra included the *Midsummer Night's Dream* Overture.

The New York Philharmonic of that day played in a rented hall called the Apollo Rooms, on lower Broadway between Canal and Walker streets. Hill wanted it to have its own building, and so the cry of "We must have a Philharmonic Hall" was first raised in 1845. It was still being echoed more than a hundred years later, until the orchestra's present home in Lincoln Center was built.

To raise money for his projected hall, Hill decided to organize a music festival. His first impulse was to invite his old teacher Ludwig Spohr to take charge, but Spohr, who was sixty years old, declined. So Hill resolved to ask Mendelssohn who, he knew, had organized successful festivals at Düsseldorf and Birmingham.

As his letter to his brother Paul shows, Felix was tempted. He had learned something about musical life in America from Maria Malibran and others who had been there, and he was always interested in new places and new audiences. But he was feeling tired and unwell. He had just ended his five years of service in Berlin to King Frederick William IV and he could think of nothing but getting away for a good long rest. Here is the letter he wrote—in English—to Ureli Corelli Hill:

> Frankfurt, January 20, 1845
> *Dear Sir:* I beg to return my best and most sincere thanks for your letter. Indeed, I may say that I felt truly proud in receiving so kind and so highly flattering an invitation, and the offer itself, as well as

the friendly words in which you couched it, will always continue a source of pride and true gratification for which I shall feel sincerely indebted to you.

But it is not in my power to accept that invitation, although I am sure it would have been the greatest treat to me if I could have done so. My health has seriously suffered during the last year, and a journey like that to your country, which I would have been most happy to undertake some three or four years ago, is at present beyond my reach. Even the shorter trips which I used to make to England or the south of Germany have become too fatiguing to me, and it will require a few years' perfect rest before I shall again be able to undertake the direction of a musical festival even in my own country. I need not tell you how much I regret to find it utterly impossible to come and to thank you in person for all the kindness and friendship which your letter contains.

Accept, then, my written thanks, which are certainly not less sincere and heartfelt, and pray let the committee know with how great a gratification and how thankfully I heard of their kind intentions toward me, and how deeply I regret not to be able to avail myself of so much kindness. Should you ever visit Europe and my country again, I hope you will not forget me and give me an opportunity of renewing your acquaintance and of expressing to you once more how deeply I feel indebted to you. I shall always remain, dear sir, yours most truly,

FELIX MENDELSSOHN BARTHOLDY

It is interesting to speculate what effect America might have had on Mendelssohn—or he on it—had he come for a visit, as Dvorak and Tchaikovsky were to do in later years. Undoubtedly the bustling atmosphere of New York in the

1840s would have fascinated him. He would have found an especially warm welcome from the German-speaking population, many of whom had organized their own music societies and choirs. He might have had a lasting effect on the New York Philharmonic's playing style, for he had the reputation of being able to bring about a rapid improvement in an orchestra in a short time.

Although he was never to make the trip, Mendelssohn kept thinking and talking about coming to America. Whenever he met an American in Europe, he brought up the subject. A young Bostonian named Bayard Taylor, who later was to become well known as a novelist and poet, called on him during his own Grand Tour of Europe. Taylor, twenty years old, thought that Felix resembled Edgar Allan Poe, with dark eyes "shining, not with a surface light, but with a pure, serene, planetary flame" and a nose that "had the Jewish prominence, without its usual coarseness. . . . the nostrils were as finely cut and flexible as an Arab's."

"As I looked upon him," Taylor confided to his memoirs, "I said to myself, 'The Prophet David!' and, since then, I have seen in the Hebrew families of Jerusalem, many of whom trace their descent from the princely houses of Israel, the same nobility of countenance."

One can only speculate on how Mendelssohn might have reacted had he known the thoughts that were running through his young visitor's mind. As it was, he politely bade him welcome and said: "You are an American. I have received an invitation to visit New York, and should like to go, but we Germans are afraid of the sea. But I may go yet: who knows? Music is making rapid advances in America; and I believe there is a real taste for the art among your people."

Taylor hastened to agree with him. Then he took out a poem he had written about Beethoven and presented it to Felix. Gravely Mendelssohn read it aloud, pronounced it very good, and asked whether he might keep the copy. In return he gave Taylor the manuscript of a chorus in his *First Wal-purgis Night* and sent him on his way rejoicing.

As he indicated in his letter to New York, Mendelssohn's health, never very robust, was now starting to deteriorate. He began to develop a nagging cough. Two weeks after declining the Philharmonic invitation, he wrote from Frankfurt to a friend: "I have for some time felt the necessity for complete rest—not traveling, not conducting, not performing. . . . It is therefore my wish to stay here quietly through winter, spring and summer, sans journeys, sans festivals, sans everything."

For a time Mendelssohn kept his promise to himself. But soon he was working hard on a work he hoped would be his masterpiece and which he planned to present in the country which had now become almost his musical home, England.

"Elijah" Triumphant

To the nineteenth century, the work that climaxed Felix Mendelssohn's career was his oratorio *Elijah*. It ranked right after Handel's *Messiah* as the world's most popular religious choral composition, and although it has slipped somewhat in total performances in recent years, it still remains a favorite of choral and singing societies.

Elijah to some extent made up for Mendelssohn's failure to write a successful opera. He kept talking about operatic plans almost to the end of his life. He told Jenny Lind that he wanted to write an opera for her. He wrote to another friend: "Give me a text I can use and I'll start working on it at 4:00 A.M. tomorrow." He took up—and discarded—a variety of possible operatic subjects. One was Shakespeare's play *The Tempest*. His failure to go ahead with this is regrettable, for the play, with its strong element of magic and fantasy, might have been just the thing for him. Another possibility was the Nibelungen legends of the ancient Germanic gods and heroes. Evidently he considered this quite seriously, because he and Fanny wrote each other letters about it. She encouraged him to try, although she thought the conclusion might present problems. "Who could finish an opera with all that horrible carnage?" she asked him. On the whole, it seems just as well that Felix left the job to Richard Wagner.

Elijah was far from an opera, but despite its religious frame-work it did offer opportunities for dramatic confrontation and musical characterization. Felix began it with the words of Elijah the Prophet to the dissolute King Ahab—"As the Lord God of Israel liveth, before whom I stand, there shall not be dew nor rain these years, but according to my word" —and followed it with an orchestral depiction of the terror of drought and famine. It was an arresting opening. There followed such graphic episodes as Elijah's raising of a wid-ow's son from the dead, his battle for the souls of the people with the false prophets of Baal, and, finally, his ascent to heaven in a fiery chariot.

Felix had had Elijah in mind as the subject for an oratorio for several years. He was a student of the Bible, as a grandson of Moses Mendelssohn might well be, and the Old Testament prophet, stern and upright, appealed to him strongly. One night Ferdinand Hiller found Mendelssohn immersed in the Bible. "Listen," Felix said, and then proceeded to read to Hiller, in a voice filled with feeling, the passage in 1 Kings 19 beginning "And behold, the Lord passed by."

"Would that not be splendid for an oratorio?" Felix ex-claimed. The chorus did become part of *Elijah*—in fact, one of the most powerful choruses Felix ever composed.

Elijah was actually written for a summer music festival in Birmingham, England. Mendelssohn had conducted in the city before. He called it "Brummagem," in the British humor-ous manner, and it was his favorite English city, after Lon-don. When Birmingham asked him to take charge of its 1846 festival and write a new work for it, he resolved to give them *Elijah*.

He had to compose it in his spare time, working early in the morning and late at night, because he was now back in Leip-zig, again directing the affairs of the Gewandhaus. The li-bretto was provided by Julius Schubring, a theologian who came from Moses Mendelssohn's home town of Dessau. Schu-

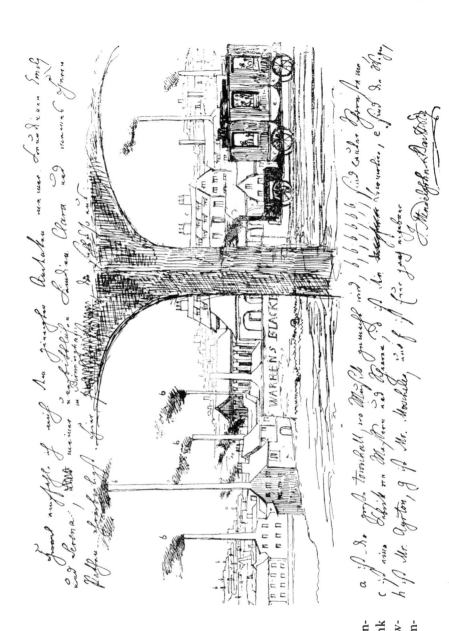

On a visit to Birmingham, Mendelssohn made this pen-and-ink sketch of the English city, showing its factories, smoky chimneys, and new railway.

bring wrote it in German and it then was translated into English, the language in which it was to be given. This was a rather awkward procedure, and *Elijah*, its Biblical passages excepted, is no great model of literary polish. But Mendelssohn found the text at least passable. And as he worked at his music, slowly and deliberately, he himself began to have the feeling that he was producing something extraordinary. "If it only turns out to be half as good as I think," he wrote to a friend, "I will be glad indeed."

Mendelssohn was in overall charge of the Birmingham Festival, with his friend Ignaz Moscheles designated as his chief assistant. Felix had the job not only of conducting *Elijah* himself, but of choosing the singers for the solo roles and overseeing the selection of the orchestra.

For the soprano soloist, Mendelssohn of course wanted Jenny Lind. He had written the part for her, tailoring it to her voice. But Jenny had never been to England, and she had commitments on the Continent that made it impossible for her to come until the following year. Disappointed, Felix had to settle for someone else.

The Birmingham authorities recommended to him a local favorite named Maria Caradori-Allen. She was Alsatian by descent, Italian by birth, forty-six years old, and had been singing in English oratorio for many—perhaps too many—years. She didn't strike Felix as much of a replacement for the youthful vibrant Jenny Lind.

Mme. Caradori-Allan didn't endear herself further to Felix when she immediately began demanding changes in her part. She particularly disliked the aria "Hear ye, Israel," which Felix had given a strong and demanding vocal line, featuring the F-sharp that Jenny Lind sang so well.

"It is not a lady's song," Mme. Caradori-Allan told him. "I would like you to transpose it down a tone."

Felix refused. He told Mme. Caradori-Allan that if she was too much of a lady to sing the aria as written, he would ask the festival authorities to replace her.

She sang it as it was. But Felix, as we shall see, had some unkind things to say about her afterward, and he did not reengage her when *Elijah* was repeated the following year in London. The other singers satisfied the composer eminently, especially a baritone named Joseph Staudigl, who sang Elijah, and a young tenor named Charles Lockey who was making his first important appearance.

The excitement in England was tremendous as Mendelssohn arrived to prepare for the performance. Somehow the word had spread that Britain's favorite composer had outdone even his past achievements and that a masterful work was to be expected.

But it was also noted that Mendelssohn did not look well. Although he was only thirty-seven, his dark hair was streaked with gray, and he seemed haggard and weary. A set of rehearsals was held in London, prior to those in Birmingham. A pupil watching Felix working with his performers at the Hanover Square Rooms reported that he "looked very worn and nervous, yet he would suffer no one to relieve him, even in the scrutiny of the orchestral parts, which he himself spread out on some of the benches . . . and insisted on sorting them out and examining for himself."

Three days before the performance, Mendelssohn went by rail to Birmingham. He always took delight in trains, which still were a novelty, and now he had his own. The trip was made in a "Mendelssohn Special," which carried Felix, Moscheles, the soloists, and a full complement of music critics.

Felix turned to one of the journalists, Henry F. Chorley of the *Athenaeum*, and said, "Now stick your claws into my work. Don't tell me what you like, but what you *don't* like."

Actually, some of the London critics had attended the preliminary rehearsals at the Hanover Square Rooms and had also examined parts of the score, so they had some advance knowledge of what the work was like. Laudatory reviews began to appear even before the first official performance.

Elijah received its world premiere in Birmingham on August 26, 1846. The time set was 11:30 A.M. and as the hour approached, the streets around the Town Hall Auditorium, which seated three thousand, were jammed with ticket holders, onlookers, and vendors of all sorts. It was a scene reminiscent of Felix's revival of the *St. Matthew Passion* in Berlin seventeen years before, when milling crowds were also unable to gain admission into the auditorium.

When Mendelssohn entered the hall to take his place, baton in hand, before the assembled forces of 125 instrumentalists, 271 choristers, and 4 solo singers, a tremendous shout went up from the packed hall. The room was lined by two rows of high windows along the sides, and just as the slender composer raised his baton to begin, the sun broke through some morning clouds and flooded into the room. One of the reporters got carried away and wrote that the light "seemed to illuminate the vast edifice in honor of the bright and pure being who stood there the idol of all beholders."

Overlooking such Victorian effusions, there is no doubt that this moment represented the apex of Felix's career. He had scored so many triumphs before, but here was one that surpassed them all. As he stood on that podium in Birmingham, his frail figure seemed to all present to represent one of the giants in musical history. If there was to be any question later as to his ultimate place, it was not raised on that sunny morning in England.

The music itself was an instantaneous and enormous success. Eight numbers—four arias and four choruses—had to be repeated, so clamorous was the applause. At the end, the *Times* reported, there were "shouts of exultation." Mendelssohn, spent by his labors and overwhelmed by the ovation, left the podium quickly, but was called back time and time again. "Never was there a more complete triumph—never a more thorough and speedy recognition of a great work of art," commented the *Times*.

Mendelssohn himself was more than satisfied with the performance, except for the unfortunate Mme. Caradori-Allan. His criticism of her is interesting because he himself was sometimes accused of writing music that was superficially smooth but lacking in underlying feeling. "The worst was the soprano part," he wrote afterward to a friend in Leipzig. "It was all so pretty, so pleasing, so elegant; at the same time so flat, so heartless, so unintelligent, so soulless, that the music acquired a sort of amiable expression about which I could go mad even today when I think about it. . . . Nothing is so unpleasant to my taste as such cold, heartless coquetry in music. It is so unmusical in itself, and yet it is often made the basis of singing and playing—making music, in fact."

On the positive side, as if to demonstrate how an interpreter can add luster to music even for its composer, he wrote to his brother Paul of Lockey's singing of "Then shall the righteous break forth": "A young English tenor sang the last air so beautifully that I was obliged to collect all my energies so as not to be affected, and to continue beating time steadily." His deepest feelings of all he conveyed in a letter to Jenny Lind: "It was the best performance that I ever heard of any of my compositions. There was so much go and swing in the way which the people played, and sang, and listened. I wish you had been there."

Mendelssohn wound up the Birmingham Festival at another concert by directing a performance of his *Midsummer Night's Dream* music. He then spent some time in London and returned to Leipzig by way of Ostende. He was so tired on the way back that he had to interrupt the journey three times just to get some sleep.

Leipzig meant more work: running the Conservatory, which was now in high gear, and taking charge of the Gewandhaus programs. He also started to write another oratorio called *Christus*. On top of all this, although nearly everyone thought *Elijah* was a splendid work as it stood, Felix decided some revisions were necessary, and started to make them.

When Cecile told him he was working too hard he replied with a smile, "Until I'm forty, I'll work; after that, I'll rest."

On February 3, 1847, Felix celebrated his thirty-eighth birthday. His family and friends gave him a musical party, which was held in the house of Moscheles, now teaching at the Leipzig Conservatory. The highlight was the enactment of the words "Gewandhaus Orchestra" in a charade. First, young Joseph Joachim, made up to look like the celebrated violin virtuoso Paganini, came out and played some variations on the G string. That was the "Ge." The "wand" (German for "wall") was represented by an enactment of the "wall scene" between Pyramus and Thisbe in *A Midsummer Night's Dream*. For the "haus," Moscheles' wife Charlotte gave a graphic imitation of a *Hausfrau*. Finally, for the "orchestra," all of the Mendelssohn and Moscheles children trooped out carrying toy instruments and noisemakers on which they proceeded to perform under Joachim's direction. Felix laughed immoderately throughout, and said afterward that it had been his finest birthday. As it turned out, it was the last he was ever to celebrate.

A few months later, Mendelssohn was back in England. A London choral society had invited him to conduct his revised *Elijah*. Felix suggested that he come over in the autumn to do it, but the sponsors wanted it in April, so once again he left Leipzig for London. He took his fifteen-year-old violin prodigy Joachim along with him, for he wished to introduce him to the British public. There was a law against children appearing professionally in England, but in deference to Mendelssohn it was ignored. Joachim played, with Felix accompanying him, and scored an immense success.

Elijah, too, was acclaimed as rapturously in London as it had been in Birmingham the previous summer. Queen Victoria and Prince Albert attended one of the performances, and afterward the latter wrote out a royal commendation for Felix, hailing him as "a second Elijah" who had "employed his genius and skill in the service of true art."

Felix had expected to be conducting *Elijah* only in London, but he somehow found himself also traveling to Birmingham and Manchester for performances there. Altogether he directed it six times in the three cities. He also gave a concert at the Philharmonic Society. Jenny Lind was now in London, her first visit there, and she came to hear him. Felix played Beethoven's Piano Concerto no. 4 in G Major. He had never been in better form. "I was desirous to play well, for there were two ladies present whom I particularly wished to please, the Queen and Jenny Lind," Felix said afterward.

A few evenings later, the positions were reversed, and Felix was in the audience listening to Jenny making her British operatic debut at Her Majesty's Theater in Meyerbeer's *Robert le Diable*. Felix didn't care much for the opera, but he thought Jenny was sensational.

His last week in London was filled with a final hectic round of musical appearances, calls on friends, receptions at the Prussian Embassy and Buckingham Palace. Everyone agreed that when he played or conducted he appeared to possess all his old vigor and freshness, but that at other times he seemed careworn and prematurely aged. When friends pressed him to stay longer in London he replied, "Ah! I wish I may not have stayed here too long! One more week of this unremitting fatigue, and I should be killed outright." At his farewell party in London, after the last musical number had been sung, he sprang to his feet, called out, "I cannot say goodbye to every one, God bless you all," and rushed from the room.

Night Song

Mendelssohn left England on May 9, 1847. He traveled via the Dover-Calais ferry, and headed toward Frankfurt, where he hoped for some months of repose with Cecile and his children.

But at the Prussian frontier town of Herbesthal near Cologne an unfortunate incident occurred. The police there were on the lookout for a certain Dr. Mendelssohn, a political radical who was associated with the German socialist and labor leader Ferdinand Lassalle. When Felix arrived they mistook him for the fugitive.

Vainly he protested that while he was indeed Dr. Mendelssohn, he was Dr. Mendelssohn the composer. At the insistence of the border guards he left the train, which continued without him. All through the day the questions flew: where had been, where was he bound, what was the purpose of his trip? He was searched. His papers were examined. He had to write out long and detailed statements describing his whereabouts for weeks past.

Legends grew up about Felix's forced stay in Herbesthal. According to one story, which was actually handed down in a Victorian biography, he was confined by the police in the village inn, and seeing an old piano there began to play his music. Recognizing the "Spring Song" from the *Songs Without*

Words, the innkeeper's daughter rushed into the room and cried, "Why, it's Felix Mendelssohn."

The story, alas, is apocryphal, but the reality was grim enough. Felix spent the whole day arguing with the bureaucrats in Herbesthal. It cost him enough time "to sketch out an overture," he later complained. Finally, with great reluctance and many suspicious looks the officials permitted him to proceed. When he finally reached Frankfurt and his family, he was almost at the point of collapse.

On his second day home Felix was handed a message from his brother Paul. He opened it, stared incredulously, uttered a cry, and fainted. His sister Fanny had died. The news was staggering not only to Felix but to the entire family. Fanny, who was forty-one years old, had given no sign of serious illness. True, she had suffered from mysterious nosebleeds for several years, but these had not been considered important. She had kept right on looking after her husband and her son Sebastian, then sixteen, and had continued composing music and staging her Sunday musicales.

The night she was taken ill, she was in the midst of rehearsing a home performance of Felix's *Walpurgis Night*. Suddenly, at the piano, she felt her arms grow numb. She was quickly put to bed, and young Sebastian Hensel was sent rushing through the dark streets to fetch a doctor. "I ran with all my might," Sebastian said later, "and kept saying to myself: 'It can't be serious; nothing bad can happen to us.'" But that night, Fanny died. The doctor said the cause had been a cerebral hemorrhage.

Her death had a fearful effect on Felix. He and his sister had been linked by unusual bonds of mutual affection and sympathy. In spirit and in mind, they almost were identical twins. When Fanny died, part of Felix died too.

Medical authorities now think that Felix probably suffered a minor stroke when he received the unexpected news of Fanny's death. Many in the Mendelssohn family seemed to suffer from a certain weakness of the blood vessels. One of these may have broken in Felix's head at the moment of stress, causing him to faint.

In any event, he never was his old cheerful, resolute self again. He tried to keep working, again resorting to "the old familiar oboes and violas . . . who live so much longer than we do," and he maintained all his family activities. But there was little heart in what he did.

Felix couldn't even bring himself to travel to Berlin for Fanny's funeral. Instead he wrote letters to all in the family expressing his grief and calling on them to be both resigned and courageous. "This will be a changed world for us all," he told Fanny's husband, "but we must try to get accustomed to the change, though by the time we do, our lives may be over, too." To his remaining sister, Rebecca, he wrote that a new chapter had now begun and added: "God will make it all right one day; this fits the beginning and end of all chapters."

That summer Felix was persuaded by Cecile that a trip to Switzerland would benefit them all. So husband and wife, together with the children, went off to Interlaken, in the Alps, where Felix so many years before had proudly written his analysis of yodeling for Professor Zelter. Paul Mendelssohn and his family and Fanny's husband and son also went along but stayed only a few weeks.

Felix and Cecile remained in Interlaken all that summer of 1847. He wandered on the mountainsides and did quite a bit of sketching. He had always been an excellent artist, and now he spent long hours making landscapes, which was much more to his taste than drawing pictures of people. He also composed a little, and produced one remarkable work—the String Quartet in F minor. It is music of agitated and emotional quality that reflects the sorrow he felt over the passing of his sister.

Occasionally a friend turned up in Interlaken. One was Henry Chorley, the British music critic who had long followed Felix's career. He and Chorley had many long talks about music. Felix expressed great interest in some of the younger composers of the day who were just beginning their careers. He particularly asked about a young Italian named Giuseppe Verdi about whom he had heard. Since Verdi had not yet written any of the great operas by which he is known today, Felix obviously was aware of the rising new star quite early. Chorley played him some of Verdi's music on the piano.

Felix himself had little opportunity to play music that summer, nor did he particularly wish to. But one day, when out for an excursion, he went for a boat ride on the Lake of Brienz. The little craft landed in a village called Ringgenberg, which was so isolated there wasn't even a decent road leading to it. Walking through its pleasant streets, Felix came upon a little church. He pushed open the door and there, in the empty building, saw a fine organ. The temptation was too great to resist. Felix found a boy near by who, for a few coins, was willing to manipulate the bellows. So there, in that empty church, Mendelssohn played the organ for an hour before returning, feeling much refreshed, to Interlaken.

A few weeks later, Felix told Chorley about the organ at Ringgenberg and asked if he would like to go there with him to hear him play it. The Englishman eagerly assented. The two friends traveled there, again by boat, and found the boy who could operate the bellows. Mendelssohn sat down at the bench and all afternoon long poured out long and rich chains of sound from the organ, starting with Bach and ending with fanciful and haunting improvisations of his own. This was the last concert ever given by Felix Mendelssohn, and it was played before an audience consisting of a solitary Englishman and the Swiss boy at the bellows in a deserted village church. "Such things must come to an end, but they are never forgotten," wrote Chorley afterward.

Chorley left this farewell picture of Felix Mendelssohn:

"My very last [remembrance] is the sight of him turning down the road, to wind back to Interlaken alone; while we turned up to cross the Wengern Alp to Grindelwald. I thought even then, as I followed his figure, looking none the younger for the loose dark coat and the wide-brimmed straw-hat bound with black crepe, which he wore, that he was too much depressed and worn, and walked too heavily. But who could have dreamed that his days on earth were so rapidly drawing to a close?"

Felix seemed somewhat better when the family returned to Leipzig after their long summer in Switzerland. He even began to work on some new musical projects, for requests and commissions were pouring in from all over Europe. The Philharmonic Society of London wanted a new symphony, the city of Liverpool a piece for the opening of a new concert hall, Frankfurt a new cantata, Cologne Cathedral another choral work for a dedicatory ceremony—the list was almost endless. Immediately ahead were performances of *Elijah* he was scheduled to conduct in Berlin and Vienna.

But first Felix decided to go to Berlin to see his brother Paul on some business matters. It was his first visit to the old house at 3 Leipzigerstrasse since Fanny's death. For Felix, it proved to be disastrous. He broke down completely. Nothing had been changed since that fateful night in May. Fanny's rooms were just as he remembered them. On the rack of the piano was the score of his *Walpurgis Night*, which she had been rehearsing when she was stricken. At these familiar sights, Felix collapsed all over again, apparently suffering another rupture of a small blood vessel. Sick and disheartened, he gave up all thought of conducting *Elijah* and returned to Leipzig. He seemed, noted one friend, "much changed in look and . . . often sat dull and listless without moving a finger."

For Felix, this was the beginning of the end. Once or twice

Mendelssohn's workroom at Leipzig in a painting made a few days after his death.

he seemed to rally a bit in spirits. On October 8 he even sat in on the entrance examinations of the new crop of students at the Conservatory, and sketched some landscapes while they were working out their problems.

The following day he walked over to visit Moscheles and his wife Charlotte at their Leipzig home. They noticed that his step lacked its former elasticity. When Charlotte asked him how he felt, Felix shrugged and answered, "Gray on gray." Moscheles suggested they go for a walk in a nearby park and Felix agreed, though not with much enthusiasm.

"Will you take me, too?" asked Charlotte.

A touch of Felix's old playfulness seemed to return, and he said to Moscheles with a smile, "What do you say? Shall we take her, too?"

The three of them walked to the park, and there Felix reminisced about his trips to England and especially about his last visit to Queen Victoria. For a time, the Moscheleses thought, he seemed almost gay.

Later that day Felix called on another old friend, a singer named Livia Frege who was married to a Leipzig lawyer. Felix had composed a new group of songs he intended to have published, and he asked her to sing them through for him to help determine their order. One was called "Night Song." Felix had composed it as a birthday present for the head of the Board of Governors of the Gewandhaus, Conrad Schleinitz. It was a strange sort of birthday gift, Felix admitted, but he said he was fond of it because it expressed his own weary and mournful frame of mind:

> *Once more the light of day is gone*
> *And ev'ning bells sound o'er the lawn,*
> *Thus travels time throughout the night,*
> *And many join his weary flight.*

Where are they now, where pleasure's art,
A friend's good cheer and faithful heart,
The sweetness in a woman's smile?—
Will none be glad with me a while?

Felix seemed moved by Livia Frege's singing of his song, and she went to get a light, so she could sing some more, for the afternoon shadows were growing. When she returned to the room, she found Felix lying on the sofa, shivering and pressing his hands to his head. He had had another attack. His limbs were cold and he had a violent headache. Nevertheless, in a little while he gathered enough strength to walk home. Cecile, alarmed by his appearance, put him promptly to bed and summoned a physician.

Nothing thereafter seemed to help, although the doctors tried every treatment they knew. Felix continued to suffer a series of similar attacks—they are now called strokes—each leaving him worse off than the one before.

As the days went by, a little group of watchers gathered around his sickbed—Cecile, his brother Paul, Moscheles, Ferdinand David and Conrad Schleinitz. Groups of people gathered in the streets around his house, and medical bulletins went out to all Europe.

On November 3, Felix suffered a stroke heavier than the others and lost consciousness. Ferdinand David saw him "hum and drum" as if music were passing through his head. Later his consciousness returned briefly, and he recognized the people in the room.

Cecile asked him if he was in pain.

"No," he replied.

"Are you tired?"

"Yes, I am tired, terribly tired," he said.

These were his last words, for after speaking them he fell into a deep and motionless sleep, like those he had had as a boy.

At 9:24 P.M. on November 4, 1847, Felix Mendelssohn died, aged thirty-eight years and eight months.

Although the silent throng outside the house had been expecting the news, they were stunned. The entire city seemed silent and lifeless that night. A young English student at the Leipzig Conservatory wrote to his family in London: "An awful stillness prevails. We feel as if the king were dead."

Much the same feeling pervaded the entire musical world. Observances and commemorations were held in practically every city with a musical organization of any size. In Leipzig the memorial concert included a performance of "Night Song," sung by Livia Frege while many in the audience openly

Deathbed drawing of Felix Mendelssohn by his brother-in-law Wilhelm Hensel.

Typical of British adulation of composer after his death is torchlight procession at Crystal Palace, London, during Mendelssohn Festival in 1860.

wept. In London the Mendelssohn commemorations went on for months, culminating almost a year later when Jenny Lind at last sang the part in *Elijah* that Felix had written for her, in a special performance at Exeter Hall.

In New York City, the Philharmonic Society gave a memorial concert with its program edged in black. The Philharmonic and other musical groups in the city also organized a special "Mendelssohn Solemnity." On February 14, 1848, some eight thousand New Yorkers assembled in black-draped Castle Garden at the Battery to do homage to the dead composer. It was one of the largest musical gatherings ever held in New York.

Messages of condolence poured in to Cecile and her children, from Queen Victoria down to ordinary music lovers in many nations. After Mendelssohn's burial in Berlin, beside the grave of Fanny, Cecile and her children retired to Frankfurt. She did not survive her husband long, however, for six years later she succumbed to consumption. A few years afterward Rebecca Mendelssohn died, also of a stroke. The only member of the family to live beyond middle age was Paul.

Felix Mendelssohn's children pursued successful careers, Carl becoming a history professor and Paul a chemist. Both his daughters married, and one moved to England. Succeeding generations continue to maintain a high level of achievement.

When the Nazis came to power in 1932, however, the Mendelssohn descendants in Germany began to suffer because of their Jewish ancestry. The bank established by Abraham and Joseph Mendelssohn more than a hundred years before was liquidated by the Reich. Many members of the family emigrated from Germany and settled as refugees in the United States, England, and Switzerland.

The Nazis also put a ban on Mendelssohn's music. Actually

some of his compositions had fallen out of favor not only in Germany but even in England, although such works as the *Italian* and *Scotch* symphonies, the Violin Concerto, and the *Midsummer Night's Dream* music never lost their popularity. Practically every composer undergoes a period of reassessment after his death. In Mendelssohn's case it became especially drastic because to many critics he represented the spirit of the Victorian age, which they were reacting against.

In Germany, the attack was led by Richard Wagner. He had been afraid to speak against Mendelssohn while he was alive; in fact, he curried his favor. But in 1850, three years after Felix's death, Wagner wrote a book called *Judaism in Music* which he published under a pseudonym, although he later acknowledged his authorship. In the book he sought to prove, using Mendelssohn as an example, that it was racially impossible for a Jew to achieve greatness in the arts.

The Nazis, of course, took Wagner's views as gospel. When Adolf Hitler took power, they expunged Mendelssohn's name from school books, tore down statues of him, and forbade performances of his music. An entire generation of Germans grew up without ever hearing a note of Mendelssohn—not even the Wedding March!

Fortunately this madness ended with the defeat of the Nazis in World War II, and Mendelssohn's music has now resumed its rightful place in German life. In fact, it seems today to be undergoing a revival of interest everywhere, with not only the basic staples being performed by leading musical organizations, as they have for more than a century, but some of the more obscure and neglected pieces being revived. If some of his music was overpraised during his lifetime, much of it was undervalued after his death. Today a balance has been restored, and we can see Mendelssohn as a composer

The Mendelssohn statue in front of the Leipzig Gewandhaus, destroyed by the Nazis as part of their campaign against the Jewish-born composer.

who wrote music that is not only consummately crafted but imbued at its best with a spirit of beauty, freshness, and the joy of youth. The great cellist Pablo Casals, who in his nineties could still feel the fascination of Mendelssohn, said, "I feel sure he will come into his own again."

In our time, perhaps he has.

Mendelssohn's Music

An entire book could easily be written analyzing Mendelssohn's music, for his output was large and encompassed nearly all the musical forms, except opera.

In this final chapter I shall discuss only a portion of his works, concentrating upon those which are most frequently played and recorded today.

SYMPHONIES

Felix wrote twelve symphonies for strings by the age of fourteen. For the most part they are light and graceful, and some are occasionally revived as a novelty.

He composed five symphonies for full orchestra, as follows: *Symphony no. 1 in C Minor, op. 11.* Written at the age of fifteen, and strongly influenced by Mozart, this nevertheless is a vigorous work with an intense and restless quality of its own. Mendelssohn scrapped its original third movement, a minuet, and replaced it with an orchestral version of the scherzo from his Octet for Strings.

Symphony no. 2 in B-flat, op. 52. This is the so-called *Lobgesang*, or "Hymn of Praise." It is more a vocal cantata than a symphony. Felix modeled it on Beethoven's Ninth Symphony, with solo singers and chorus. Actually, the final choral movement is as long as the first three instrumental movements combined. This makes it seem unbalanced. Although it was once highly popular, it is seldom performed nowadays.

Symphony no. 3 in A Minor, Scotch, *op. 56*. Felix's love for Scotland shines through this symphony. However, it is more of an impression than a literal depiction of the Scottish landscape. The second movement opens with a lilting clarinet solo which is a bit reminiscent of the song "Charlie Is My Darling." The dramatic last movement has been described both as a wild highland fling and a gathering of warlike clans. The final coda is regarded by some critics as somewhat trite and pompous, but other listeners find it stirring. The *Scotch* Symphony has been made into a colorful ballet by George Balanchine.

Symphony no. 4 in A Major, Italian, *op. 90*. The *Italian* is commonly accepted as the masterpiece among Mendelssohn's symphonies. Lucid and sunny in spirit, it is also brilliantly orchestrated and tightly constructed. It is more pictorial than the *Scotch*, with strong echoes of a religious procession in the second movement, and a wild popular dance, a Neapolitan *saltarello*, in the fourth. This is a young man's musical picture of Italy, fashioned with skill, sensitivity, and exuberance.

Symphony no. 5 in D Minor, Reformation, *op. 107*. Despite its high opus number, this was completed before the symphonies nos. 3 and 4. It was published only after Mendelssohn's death. A Protestant religious coloration is given by Luther's chorale "A Mighty Fortress Is Our God" and the "Dresden Amen," a rising theme that Wagner later used in his opera *Parsifal*. It is a less cohesive and consistent work than either the *Scotch* or *Italian* symphonies. Nevertheless, it has been appearing with increasing frequency on symphonic programs in recent years.

Incidental Music to "A Midsummer Night's Dream," opp. 21 and 61.

The complete *Midsummer Night's Dream* music includes

thirteen numbers, of which the best known are the Overture, Scherzo, Song ("You Spotted Snakes"), Intermezzo, Nocturne, Wedding March, Dance of the Clowns, and Finale. The famous opening E major woodwind chords of the Overture set the enchanted mood of the entire work, and also bring it to a close. Note how the magical effect is heightened when the third of the four chords unexpectedly shifts to A minor.

Writers from Mendelssohn's time to our own have found the personalities of Shakespeare's play reflected vividly in the music, including the regal pair Oberon and Titania, the four bewildered lovers, the mischievous Puck, and the stagestruck country bumpkins, including Bottom, whose donkey braying is graphically represented by an unwieldy instrument, the ophicleide.

But picturesque as the music is, it can be enjoyed equally for its dreamlike atmosphere and sheer beauty of sound, for seldom have so many exquisite melodies and subtle orchestral colorations been compressed into about an hour's listening time.

Concert performances of the complete score are infrequent, with only the Overture usually turning up on concert programs. And while the Wedding March is heard often enough, the honors are usually done by a church organist, which robs the music of its orchestral brilliance.

Fortunately, the full musical score is readily available in recordings. It sometimes may be heard "live" at ballet performances, such as George Balanchine's beautiful version of the *Midsummer Night's Dream* by the New York City Ballet Company.

Violin Concerto in E Minor, op. 64.

This is the sort of work that, all by itself, justifies a composer's life. The Mendelssohn E Minor probably is the most popular of all violin concertos, and with good reason. Aside from its eloquent and superbly violinistic melodies, it was a boldly innovative work for its time and exerted an influence on subsequent violin concertos of the romantic period. The violin itself sings out the first theme, dispensing with the usual orchestral introduction. The cadenza for the soloist is an essential element of the first movement, bridging the way from the development section to the recapitulation, rather than serving as a mere virtuoso showpiece. The entire work is designed to be played without pause, although audience applause often drowns out the solitary bassoon note, a sustained B, which links the first and second movements.

OVERTURES

Hebrides, or *Fingal's Cave, op. 26.* This remarkable work opens with a short rhythmic figure in the lower strings and bassoon that admirably suggests the restless surge of the sea. The entire work seems to grow out of this haunting phrase. The more lyric second theme was described by a famous musical writer, Donald F. Tovey, as "quite the greatest melody Mendelssohn ever wrote." Although the Overture lasts only about ten minutes, its shifting rhythms, ceaseless motion, and color-flecked orchestration convey a uniquely vivid and spacious musical image of the sea.

Calm Sea and Prosperous Voyage, op. 27. Although the ripple of the waves also imbues this work with a nautical spirit, the mood is less realistic than in the *Hebrides* Overture. At the end, trumpet fanfares welcome the voyagers to port.

Fair Melusine, op. 32. Once again, sea fever pervades a Mendelssohn overture, this time inspired by a legend about a woman who was half serpent. The flowing opening theme was later adopted by Richard Wagner for the Prelude to his own aqueous opera, *Das Rheingold.*

Ruy Blas, op. 95. Though Felix himself later professed disdain for this piece, it provides a sweeping dramatic introduction for a romantic play by Victor Hugo about a valet who loved a queen in seventeenth-century Spain.

PIANO MUSIC

In his mature years, Felix wrote two piano concertos, of which the first, in G minor, op. 25, is still fairly frequently performed. Although not on a level with the Violin Concerto, it is a pleasant if rather sentimental work, with warm melodies, brilliant keyboard writing and a neat, well-balanced structure. Played with verve, it can make for enjoyable listening.

Of Felix's works for solo piano, the meatiest is the *Variations sérieuses* in D minor, op. 54, a set of seventeen variations. The theme itself is brief and melancholy, the variations terse and compact. The piece shows the influence of Bach, with a good deal of power compressed into the twelve minutes or so it takes to play.

Of the many lighter pieces Felix wrote for piano, the *Songs Without Words* constitute a unique library of what might be called musical Victorianism. For years young English maidens tinkled out these pieces on their drawing-room spinets. Sir Arthur Conan Doyle's great detective Sherlock Holmes played them on his violin to soothe Dr. Watson's nerves. They have made favorite encore pieces for pianists from Vladimir Horowitz to Emil Gilels. All together Mendelssohn wrote eight books of six songs each, two of which were published after his death. However hackneyed such pieces as "Spring Song," "Spinning Song," and the several "Venetian Gondola" songs may be, their durability under years of maltreatment argues well for their intrinsic worth.

CHAMBER MUSIC

This is an area of Mendelssohn's music undeservedly neglected today. He wrote a number of fine string quartets, and two trios for piano, violin, and cello. One of these, in D minor, was selected by cellist Pablo Casals for a performance in the White House before President John F. Kennedy in 1961. A unique chamber music masterpiece is the Octet in E-flat, op. 20, scored for double string quartet, which Felix wrote at sixteen. The best description of it remains that by his sister Fanny, quoted in chapter 4.

Vocal and Choral Music

While he never equaled his friend Robert Schumann in the imaginativeness and sensitivity of his *Lieder*, Mendelssohn wrote many songs of great fluency and charm. His "On Wings of Song" has proved as appealing—and as durable—as any of his piano *Songs Without Words*. The famous carol "Hark! the herald-angels sing" was adapted from a tune he wrote for a Gutenberg Festival in Leipzig in 1840. Perhaps most moving of all is his *Nachtlied*, the "Night Song" he wrote just before his death—not only because of the circumstances of its composition, but because it is an eloquent and solemn expression of the resignation he felt.

Of Felix's two oratorios, *St. Paul* and *Elijah*, the former has all but passed from the scene, although it possesses several noble choruses. *Elijah*, however, remains a favorite of many choral groups and church organizations. This is not always to its advantage, because many performers approach it with an overly reverential "oratorio style." The result is that it often seems stodgy and undramatic, which was the last thing Mendelssohn wanted. With a brisk and forceful conductor, and top-quality singers and instrumentalists, *Elijah* can still be a thrilling experience.

Ballet has given a new relevance to Mendelssohn's music for modern audiences. Below, a scene from George Balanchine's production of *A Midsummer Night's Dream* for the New York City Ballet Company. Below right, Patricia McBride as Titania in the same production in a scene with the transfigured Bottom. Above right, Mendelssohn's *Scotch* Symphony with Robert Maiorano, Sara Leland, and Earle Sieveling.

Throughout his life Mendelssohn wrote a series of short piano pieces called *Songs Without Words*. Published in England, they became the favorite musical fare of a generation of Victorians who played them in their own homes. In all, there were forty-eight. This is the first of them, Op. 19, No. 1, in Felix's original draft. Observe the precision of his musical handwriting, which many of his friends compared to printed notes.

A Note on Recordings

Much of Mendelssohn's music has been recorded, although several areas, such as his songs and chamber music, have been rather neglected. Many of the most popular works have been released in a multiplicity of versions. Following are recommended recordings of some of the works mentioned in this book. All of the records below were listed as currently available in the January 1972 issue of the *Schwann Record & Tape Guide*.

Elijah—Rafael Fruhbeck de Burgos conducting soloists, chorus, and New Philharmonia Orchestra (Angel).
—Eugene Ormandy conducting soloists, Philadelphia Orchestra, and Singing City Choirs (RCA).

The First Walpurgis Night—Frederick Waldman conducting soloists and Musica Aeterna Orchestra and Chorus (Decca).

Hebrides Overture—see Symphony no. 3.

Midsummer Night's Dream, Incidental Music—Rafael Fruhbeck de Burgos conducting soloists, chorus, and New Philharmonia Orchestra (London).
—Peter Maag conducting soloists, chorus, and London Symphony Orchestra (London).

Octet in E-flat for Strings—Academy of St. Martin-in-the-Fields (Argo).

Piano Concerto no. 1 in G Minor—Joseph Kalichstein, pianist, with London Symphony Orchestra conducted by André Previn. Includes *Variations sérieuses* (RCA).
—Rudolf Serkin, pianist, with Philadelphia Orchestra conducted by Eugene Ormandy. Includes *Piano Concerto no. 2 in D Minor* (Columbia).

Symphony no. 1 in C Minor—Louis Lane conducting Cleveland Orchestra (Columbia).
—Wolfgang Sawallisch conducting New Philharmonia Orchestra. Includes *Symphony no. 2* (Philips).

Symphony no. 2 in B-flat, Lobgesang—Wolfgang Sawallisch conducting soloists and New Philharmonia Orchestra. Includes *Symphony no. 1* (Philips).

Symphony no. 3 in A Minor, Scotch—Leonard Bernstein conducting New York Philharmonic. Includes *Hebrides Overture* (Columbia).
—Peter Maag conducting London Symphony Orchestra. Includes *Hebrides Overture* (London).

Symphony no. 4 in A Major, Italian—Leonard Bernstein conducting New York Philharmonic (Columbia).
—Lorin Maazel conducting Berlin Philharmonic Orchestra. Includes *Symphony no. 5* (Deutsche Grammophon).

Symphony no. 5 in D Minor, Reformation—Leonard Bernstein conducting New York Philharmonic (Columbia).
—Lorin Maazel conducting Berlin Philharmonic Orchestra. Includes Symphony no. 4 (Deutsche Grammophon).

Trio no. 1 in D Minor and no. 2 in C Minor—Beaux Arts Trio (Philips).

Variations sérieuses in D Minor—Joseph Kalichstein, pianist. Includes *Piano Concerto no. 1* (RCA).

Violin Concerto in E Minor—Pinchas Zukerman, violinist with New York Philharmonic conducted by Leonard Bernstein (Columbia).

Index

ILLUSTRATION ACKNOWLEDGMENTS

Courtesy, Professor Felix Gilbert, Princeton, N.J.: pp. 7, 125; from London Illustrated News, *May, 1860: pp. 152–153; Copyright Mendelssohn Archive, Staatsbibliothek, Berlin: pp. 17 (both), 19, 45, 62, 69, 100, 109, 148, 151, 156; from Hermann Meyer,* Universum, *New York, 1852: p. 68; from Felix Moscheles (trans. and ed.),* Letters of Felix Mendelssohn to Ignaz and Charlotte Moscheles, *Boston, 1888: pp. 60, 81 (both), 97, 136, 166; Muller Collection in Special Collections of Music Division, Research Library of Performing Arts, The New York Public Library at Lincoln Center, Astor, Lenox and Tilden Foundations: p. 126; Courtesy, New York City Ballet (Photographs by Martha Swope): pp. 164, 165 (both); Picture Collection, The New York Public Library: pp. 4, 13, 79, 95; from the Scribner Art Files: pp. 23, 75; from J. Stieler,* The Great German Composers, *London, 1879: p. 27.*